Antique & Collectible Pyrography ★ Burnt Wood
THE BURNING PASSION

by
Carole and Richard Smyth

©1995
Carole and Richard Smyth

ISBN# 0-89538-026-9

©Copyright 1995 by Carole and Richard Smyth
L-W Book Sales

All rights reserved. No part of this work may be reproduced
or used in any forms or by any means - graphic, electronic, or
mechanical, including photocopying or storage and retrieval
systems - without written permission from the copyright holder.

Published by: L-W Book Sales
P.O. Box 69
Gas City, IN 46933

Please write for our free catalog.

Attention Collectors . . . if you would like to contribute photographs,
information, or your collection (possibly for profit), please call L-W Books
(toll free) at 1-800-777-6450 Tuesday thru Friday 9 A.M. to 3 P.M.

Layout and Design by Amy Van Hoosier

Preface

At the turn of this century women's magazines were promoting pyrography, in glowing terms, as a new pastime suitable for ladies. Fueled by technical innovation and fanned by the art supply companies, pyrography quickly became a burning passion for thousands of ladies. Their skill and artistry changed a fad into an art form as American pyrography developed its own unique identity.

One hundred years later interest in pyrography has been rekindled by a growing number of collectors. This book provides the beginning collector or dealer with a basic understanding of this rediscovered medium. The photographs will help develop your 'eye' so that you may establish your own sense of values to enable you to collect or trade with confidence.

This book will cover:

* the development of equipment and techniques that made Victorian pyrography an exciting new media for artists

* the social factors that made pyrography such popular home craft

* how pyrography developed to include paint decoration and simple wood carving

* how the hobby was promoted by the art supply and mail order companies

* how to identify hand done pyro-etching from factory stamping

* how to recognize and name the various background patterns.

* how to establish a basic provenance

* evaluation of quality and value

* how to use the price guide

* why reproductions are not a problem

* how to clean and make simple repairs

* why now is a great time to start collecting pyrography

All of the articles illustrated are from "The Carole Smyth Collection" and we are grateful to the many dealers and collectors who have helped us over the years and for the generous way they have shared their knowledge. Special thanks are due to Lorraine and John Buckley for their enthusiastic encouragement to write this book and for finding several of our favorite pieces. To Rosa Newcomer of Covered Bridge Antiques, Denver, PA, who runs the friendliest antique mall on Route 272.

Finally we would like to thank Dutch Shultz of Federal Hill Booksellers for introducing us to Scott Wood of L-W Book Sales, our very "writer friendly" publishers.

Introduction

Pyrography is part of our common heritage. There are many theories about its origin from Flemish artists who painted on wood instead of canvas and sketched the outlines for their paintings by burning lines, to men in taverns, sitting and drinking by the fireside and amusing themselves by drawing designs with a hot poker. There may be some truth to all these romantic notions but pyrography has probably been in existence since mankind discovered uses for fire. Its initial form may have been nothing more than a design, picture or message burnt into wood as an easy alternative to carving.

We do know that in the early 1800's pyrography enjoyed a brief popularity before it was rediscovered about 1880 by another new development, the women's magazine. From then until the early twenties, pyrography, in America, changed from a simple pleasure for men with time on their hands, to an expression of burning desire for thousands of Victorian ladies. They celebrated their new found freedoms by putting down the sewing needle and picking up the red hot stylus. Fanciful designs were burned on the many thousands of wooden boxes, wall plaques and small pieces of furniture purchased from factories that sprang up to fuel this exciting craze for self expression.

Some of the results are truly beautiful. Their handiwork provides us with a unique insight of their changing life-styles and attitudes from Victorian prim through the gay 90's to the roaring twenties. From the saucy picture of a lady exposing her ankles on a beach, through the rituals of courtship, to favorite fruits and flowers and even apparent amusement at the sight of a puppy being punished with a muzzle. All these images were themes for decorating furniture and the myriad of paraphernalia considered so essential to the Victorian home. Like many other antique lovers we had often admired the spirit and romanticism of their handiwork but, for years, never made the commitment to purchase or collect.

This changed the day we went to Brimfield, the village in Massachusetts that three times a year becomes the center of the world for antique dealers and collectors. We were looking for a house warming gift for a friend in England. It had to compliment his decor, an eclectic combination of Victorian, country pine and Arts and Crafts. We wanted something very American, hand crafted and hopefully, not put too big a dent in our budget. In the very first booth we both pounced on a tie rack decorated with a Gibson Girl *and* an Indian Chief. It was perfect! In that instant we realized we had discovered our next collection.

At day's end we were tired and happy. Our pockets were empty but our bags were full of Flemish Art, poker work, burnt wood or pyrography. It seemed every dealer had a different name for it. On returning home and spreading our purchases on the kitchen table, we began to appreciate that not all pyrography is created equal. Time had not been kind to some pieces and in others the artistry was less than inspiring.

Several years later we are more discerning and have learned to separate factory stamping from the creativity of a skilled artist. Our own collection now concentrates on pieces that combine pyrography with paint decoration although we still appreciate those examples where the passion of the burned design says it all.

Table of Contents

American Pyrography

Origins of Style	6
Social Factors	8
The New Technology	9
The Techniques	13
The Manufacturers and Art Supply Companies	19
Identifying Manufacturers	20
How to Evaluate Workmanship and Assess Value	34
Backgrounds	36
Care and Repair	37
Pieces and Prices	38
Furniture and Major Pieces	39
Things That Should or Could Be Hung	48
Smoking and Drinking	72
Games People Play	77
For the Office?	79
To Adorn Your Table and Impress Guests	85
And So To Bed	89
You Name It, There Was A Box for It!	91
Burned Leatherwork	105

American Pyrography
Origins of Style

In America, pyrography became a unique art form because it took full advantage of the Victorian developments in technology to interpret the new forms of design and social values that emerged through the Edwardian Era until its demise in the early twenties. Although its popularity actually peaked during the Edwardian Era this hobby epitomized the spirit and style of the Late Victorian age.

A. BEFORE
This piece of pyrography dates from 1819. The style is very formal and stilted. The short time available while the iron needle was hot allowed only a basic point A to point B approach to outlining.

B. DURING
Just a couple of whisk broom holders but they typify the two aspects of pyrography at the turn of the century.

The one with the lady's head is finely burned and colored with a delicate touch and the plain background is "enhanced" with glass jewels. The back of the holder provides impact with all over deep burned detail as a background to the holly leaves. Overall, a nice piece of handiwork that required a lot of time to complete.

The other holder is a factory creation. The complex background and the flower design stamped or scorched in the factory. Only the painting and varnishing were done at home. Instant pyrography!

C. AFTER
This is incredibly fine work both in burning and coloring. Signed MN '55 it was almost certainly produced with an electric heated stylus which allowed very fluid lines but no variation on depth of burn because the temperature of the electrically heated point cannot be changed while producing a line. Nobody has the time to produce burned backgrounds anymore.

A

B

C

Social Factors

By the late 1800's, spare time and money were becoming available as America developed into one of the most industrialized nations in the world. Railroads crisscrossed the States and a postal service delivered all manner of wonderful catalogs and periodicals. This opened up a new world of possibilities not only to women in thriving industrial cities like New York, Boston and Chicago but also their sisters in the newly prospering country towns where local stores and services were making their lives a litter easier.

For decades, out of necessity, women had pieced scraps of material together fashioning them into quilts to keep their families warm. They had learned to weave, knit and crochet clothing and other "comforts" to make life easier. They made bedding and table coverings often with wondrous results when they had the time or money to let their creativity take hold and their yearnings for color and design brighten their often utilitarian homes.

Women were already actively engaged in making feather pictures, decorating china, weaving hair into jewelry and making domes of dried flowers, mosses and butterflies. Imagine the joy, when thumbing through the latest Sears Catalogue, of discovering a new pastime. Here was a new challenge, *burning wood then painting it*. Uncle Silas would now have a new pipe rack, hand made and decorated for his birthday. Grandma Sophie could be given a sewing box adorned with pretty flowers, just like the ones in her garden. If you were not too proficient with a "hot needle" you could buy a stamped or pre-burnt box and still personalize it by painting.

Prior to the turn of the century pyrography was more commonly known as Burnt Wood or Poker Decoration, a pastime with European origins where men used pokers, heated in fires, as instruments to burn simple designs or messages onto wood.

The New Technology

The large size of the poker made intricate work virtually impossible. Attempts to produce a miniature version initially floundered as the loss of size resulted in the point losing its heat too rapidly to enable the production of a long continuous line. The constant reheating made the completion of any large work extremely tedious.

The most popular solution became known as the Platinum Point. The point was a tube made of a platinum-iridium alloy that resembled a hollow fountain pen nib. It was kept hot by burning a benzine/air mixture supplied through a rubber tube from a glass atomizer. A hand held rubber bulb was squeezed to supply air to the point of combustion and this controlled the rate and depth of burning by varying the temperature of the point. The point fitted into a handle insulated with cork and advanced users could alter the width and character of the lines by changing the size and shape of the point, in much the same way a calligrapher changes nibs in a pen. These new instruments required dexterity and flair to produce the best results, allowing pyrography to become an ideal pastime for the ladies of the house.

Within a few years a new industry was established to supply Pyrography Kits and hundreds of different work pieces either by mail order or from local general stores.

The most ambitious pyrographers not only created their own designs but also made the work pieces. The art supply companies soon realized that there was a market for blanks that were pre stamped with outlines for the less artistic hobbyist to follow. Using the same technology that was currently being used for marking shipping crates, the designs were either printed, scorched into the wood or stamped with the impression colored with brown ink to simulate the finished product. Many of these stamped pieces remain today and even though they may never have been burned by hand are still collected as examples of pyrography. Frequently the purchaser decorated these factory pieces by painting. This practice was encouraged by the supply houses as this allowed the more timid to participate without the discomforts of burning the wood.

The hobby was not without its health hazards. The 1907 Flemish Art Company Instruction manual indicates conditions that would make today's safety and indoor air quality advocates blanch. Benzine was an early form of gasoline and the many references in the early instruction manuals to the prevention of explosions indicates that they must have occurred with some regularity. A small handful of asbestos was placed in the benzine bottle to reduce the chance of explosion. Today asbestos is virtually banned because of its known cause of cancer, particularly when combined with smoke and you cannot have pyrography without smoke. The Flemish Art Co. sold a Patented Smoke Blower that was guaranteed to blow the smoke away from the eyes.

By the fall of 1908, the Sears Roebuck catalog was offering a safer, Gas Jet Outfit which was comprised of a wooden knob for fitting over a household gas jet together with five feet of rubber tubing connected to a wooden handle with a special burning point. In 1910 this design was refined by adding a device to regulate the heat and was marketed as the Gas o'Pen. By 1910 Sears also offered The Alco Fountain Burning Instrument which had a nickel point that used less explosive denatured alcohol.

Collecting these early pyrography kits would be a real challenge but a lot of fun. Not many seem to have survived intact. The rubber bulbs and tubing have nearly always become very hard and brittle but modern bulbs and tubing are available but we strongly warn you against trying to use old kits.

Modern pyrography points are heated by electricity and resemble a small soldering iron, but considering the current concern with secondhand cigarette smoke, it is unlikely that pyrography would be a socially acceptable activity in many homes today.

Whatever equipment was used, the most popular wood for burning designs was Basswood because it has a very even grain. This is very important as the burning point can traverse the grain without the burnt line 'jumping' and becoming uneven. Basswood is just a little harder than pine, is easy to carve and its light cream color, combined with the even grain, allows it to take stains or colors very well. With age the unfinished wood tends to turn to an attractive, medium gingery brown. Other woods used included maple, holly and satinwood. Any woods containing rosin were found to be unsuitable as the burning rosin would contaminate the hot platinum point.

- **D.** This is ALL you need to produce a pyrography masterpiece.
- **E.** Handkerchief box with design printed in ink ready to burn. This is how they came from the manufacturer.
- **F.** Platinum Points and the instructions that came wrapped around the point in wooden vials.
- **G.** A great tin with deadly contents. 100% asbestos and they sold it as a safety feature! Who knew?

D

E

F

G

THAYER & CHANDLER, CHICAGO.

Peerless Pyrographic Outfits

These Outfits contain the most complete assortment of material used in Pyrographic decoration. In addition to the principal articles required for burning, they contain Pelican Instruction Book, Liquid Water Color Outfit, Pyro-ebony, Trans. Pyro-varnish, Painting and Staining Brushes and Peerless patent Cork Handles with controlling device, by means of which the heated point can be regulated perfectly for steady low, medium or high temperature burning.

Consisting of large imported double rubber bulb with long tubing, benzine bottle with wire hook, glass top alcohol lamp, rubber tubing, Peerless patent cork handle, metal union cork, liquid water color outfit, ¼ pint Pelican varnish, 1-6 pint Pelican ebony, 1 water color brush. 1 varnish brush, Pelican instruction book, 3 pieces stamped practice wood and platinum point as designated below. All contained in well finished box stamped with design suitable for decorating.

Set	Each
101—Contains Phoenix Point No. 38	$5.00
102—Contains Phoenix Point No. 41	5.25
103—Contains Pelican Point No. 21	5.75
104—Contains Pelican Point No. 3	6.00
105—Contains Pelican Point No. 7	6.50

Extra Large Imported Double Rubber Bulb substituted in above Outfits, 50c extra.

Standard Pyrographic Outfits

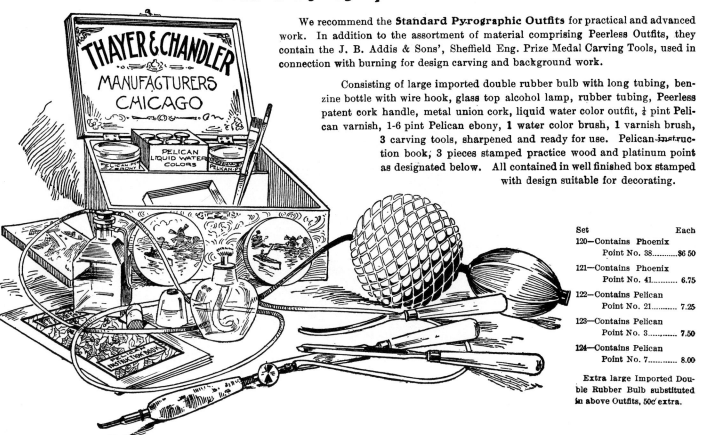

We recommend the **Standard Pyrographic Outfits** for practical and advanced work. In addition to the assortment of material comprising Peerless Outfits, they contain the J. B. Addis & Sons', Sheffield Eng. Prize Medal Carving Tools, used in connection with burning for design carving and background work.

Consisting of large imported double rubber bulb with long tubing, benzine bottle with wire hook, glass top alcohol lamp, rubber tubing, Peerless patent cork handle, metal union cork, liquid water color outfit, ¼ pint Pelican varnish, 1-6 pint Pelican ebony, 1 water color brush, 1 varnish brush, 3 carving tools, sharpened and ready for use. Pelican instruction book, 3 pieces stamped practice wood and platinum point as designated below. All contained in well finished box stamped with design suitable for decorating.

Set	Each
120—Contains Phoenix Point No. 38	$6.50
121—Contains Phoenix Point No. 41	6.75
122—Contains Pelican Point No. 21	7.25
123—Contains Pelican Point No. 3	7.50
124—Contains Pelican Point No. 7	8.00

Extra large Imported Double Rubber Bulb substituted in above Outfits, 50c extra.

Pelican Instruction Book explains how to decorate each article for decoration listed in this catalog. Price 25c.

The Techniques

The basic skill that had to be mastered to produce pyrography has always been Outlining. The following extracts of a 1903 publication, "A Treatise on the Art of Wood Burning" by A.L. Danzinger describes the method and suitable exercises for using the kits and printed articles.

A Treatise on the Art of Wood Burning

OUTLINING

THE student having accomplished the strokes so as to be able to make a clean cut line without the dots or holes, can now take some design like the illustration *C* and *D* to cut 2, page 12 and try outlining.

In outlining a design it is advisable to burn on the right side of your drawing as shown on section 3. page 12.by the points *b* and *c*. By following this rule you keep the inside of your design clean and white, and are not so liable to scorch the edges of your drawing.

Always keep turning your article so to make the outline to the right and never cross over to the left, as shown in cut *a*, section 3, page 12, as by doing so there is a possibility of the small escape hole scorching your drawing.

For delicate lining hold the point higher up, so that the tip end strikes the wood, and press the rubber bulb gently, while for heavy, deep lining increase the pressure on the bulb, *but not on the point,* holding the point lower down so as to strike its broadest part.

When working on some woods, where the grain is rather hard and stands out, the point should not be passed over the surface too quickly or it will jump the grain and give the lines a very irregular and ragged appearance.

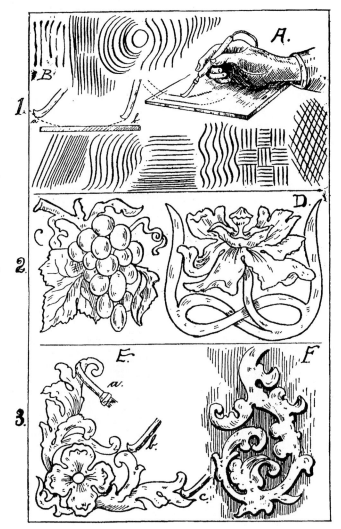

This is the picture that is referred to as being on page 12 in the article *OUTLINING*.

The supply companies encouraged pyrographers to enhance their work by coloring between the burnt lines with stains, water colors or oil paints. To make sure artists bought coloring kits just for pyrography, the suppliers provided special labeling and sold these products as new developments as can be seen from the following extract from the Flemish Art Company Catalog of 1907.

COLORING AND SHADING

STAINS.—Where a plain color without shading is desired use the "Flemish Art Pyrographic Stains."

These are mixed with a secret preparation which prevents the colors from spreading or running and therefore very easy to use and satisfactory.

Simply apply the color desired with a soft brush, letting it dry; if not dark enough apply a second coat.

WATER COLORS.—For shading use water colors; either the half pan or tube colors may be used to good advantage, but the "Flemish Art Sets" of either have specially adapted colors for pyrographic work, and if used insure the bright crisp effects so often admired in pyrographic art objects, yet so seldom obtained by the amateur on account of not having proper materials.

The Flemish Art sets of half pan or tube colors are put up with special care and are furnished with the proper brushes for applying to Pyro work. When using these colors in either style be sure not to use too much water; just dilute enough to make colors spread easily and smoothly.

Use special care in blending colors or in shading to blend from the darkest part of the work to the lightest, or from the shadows to the high lights.

For shading from a dark color to obtain darker effects use ivory black, blending from the darkest part as above.

If, after applying the first coat, it is not brilliant enough, apply a second coat over the first, blending carefully as before from dark to light.

The Thayer & Chandler Catalog of the same year was touting the advantages of lacquer over the water colors:

"Thayer and Chandler's Japanese Lacquer is specially prepared for tinting the inside of all articles where the wood has been cut across the grain such as round, oval, heart, and all fancy shaped boxes, hair receivers, tobacco jars, nut bowls etc. This stain will not allow the wood to expand and lose its shape as is the case when water stains are used."

One of the restrictions of using large, thin sheets of basswood was its tendency to warp which led to the introduction of plywood. The first plywood was constructed of only three plies or layers of wood, the center one being thicker than the two outer shells. The plies were glued together with the grain of the outer plies set at right angles to the center ply. Thus when the wood got damp the outside plies would counteract the warpage of the inner ply and the wood would remain flat. All the supply houses filled pages of their catalogs with examples of Three Ply Basswood and this development would later to prove to be of national importance when it became widely used as a material for building airplanes.

Techniques were developed to produce three dimensional effects. These were known as relief, undercutting or carved effects but these early methods were time consuming and difficult to control. The skill needed to produce a clean edge can be appreciated for Danzinger's instructions.

A Treatise on the Art of Wood Burning

SEMI-RELIEF OR UNDERCUTTING

THIS is a process by which the design when finished is made to stand out in bold relief. This is usually done after the student has finished the outlining and background; He then goes over the outlines on the shaded and under parts of the design, holding the point on a slight angle so that in re-marking the line, as if the idea was to cut underneath the design, keeping the point at a white heat and moving it slowly. In this manner the outlines are concaved and made deeper and broader, which tends to place the entire design in relief at the same time smoothing and cutting off any ragged edges left by making the background.

DESIGN FOR PLAQUE

A Treatise on the Art of Wood Burning

BOLD RELIEF AND CARVED EFFECTS

ALTHOUGH of a much bolder character than ordinary burning, yet it may be applied to a large variety of articles, both small and large. It may be broadly described as carving by means of a red hot knife.

The method of burning in the outlines is exactly the same described in semi-relief work.

Before filling in the details of the design, it is advisable to burn away the background from the drawing outward to the depth of one eight of an inch or more, with the point at a white heat, stroking with a chopping stroke. Keep stroking and re-stroking over each stroke until the depth of carving is acquired, pulling away from the outlines outward and decreasing the depth of outer edge. It is unnecessary to burn the entire background to a depth of one eight inch or more, except on small articles. Large pieces like plaques to panels of studies, one to one and a half inch from around the design is sufficient, and the depth of carving can diminish to the outer edges of the articles.

The bellows can be forced to keep the point as its whitest heat and burn slowly. *Do not bear upon the point.*

In 1907 the Flemish Art Company took advantage of plywood to produce a simple carved relief effect known as "The New Three Ply Panel Carving Process." They introduced this development with the following Instructions.

Before Carving

After Carving

THE NEW 3-PLY PANEL CARVING PROCESS

is the latest edition to Pyrography and can be utilized to further enhance the beauty of Pyrographic work by the artistic results which are obtained with very little labor and in a short space of time. The process is simple and as follows:

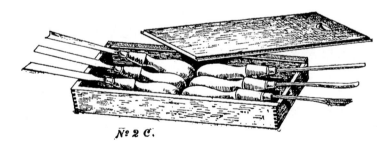
Nº 2 C.

Carving Set

The tools necessary for this purpose are six easily handled chisels, as per drawing, and are furnished in two styles, the main difference being in their length. The No. 1 is 5 1/2 inches long, from handle top to end of chisel; the No. 2 is 8 inches long. The first operation necessary for panel carving is to cut a frame or edge all around the panel at least an inch wide, or wider in proportion to panel or design, then follow the design on panel as closely as possible, **cut to depth of first layer of wood only,** being careful to cut evenly as to depth. For this first operation use chisel or knife with edge at an angle, holding it firmly in hand.

The second operation consists of **lifting out the first** ply of the wood, to which depth design and frame have been cut; this is done with the flat chisel. Insert to depth of cut, press down and forward and the first layer lifts out, and your carved design is before you. Then clean out the edges of design carefully.

The round chisels or gouges, as they are called, are then used if design is fruits or flowers to round off edges of leaves, or if a scene or group to deepen lines of faces, deepen eyes, etc., etc. When this is done burn panels in regular way and color. Burn backgrounds in panels rather dark; use the oak shading style of background shading for the frame you have left, to contrast with the background of the panel and show up the design beautifully. To properly carve a panel takes no longer than five to twenty minutes, according to how intricate the design may be.

Any three-ply article can be carved as above.

Some Three-ply Panels that are Very Effective When Carved

Danzinger's booklet also describes two other techniques that were available for the accomplished pyrographer. Scorching and Pyro-etching.

Scorching was used to shade in areas particularly when the piece was not going to be colored. Areas were darkened by using a point with a flat side heated to a dull red and gently drawn across the grain of the wood. By controlling the temperature and speed the point would produce various shades of brown. This technique required a very deft touch and is sometimes used to provide shading faces or the sails of ships.

Pyro-etching is similar too, but requires more skill than outlining. There are no pre stamped lines to follow and a fine point is used to produce a freehand picture or design, just like a pen and ink artist would draw on paper. There was no background work so the wood was left clean with the possible exception of a few sketchy lines to relieve the bareness.

As a final method of embellishment, the art supply companies sold specially designed pieces with instructions printed on them to encourage the hobbyist to buy and use:

> "Brilliant Glass Jewels to add luster and give luxurious finish to beads, necklaces, belts and colored spangles of metal to decorate head-dresses and as dew on leaves and flowers."

This technique does not appear to have been very popular. *Who says the Victorians didn't know when enough was enough?* Few examples exist today where all the "jewels" are still in place.

Pyrography was also promoted as a decoration for leather, cardboard and various textiles such as Naan, (a material similar to plush velvet.) Very few examples of work on cardboard or Naan exist today but there are enough examples of burnt leather work to provide the basis for a rewarding collection. Many small leather articles can be found but the burned designs were usually applied in a factory using a hot stamp, just like branding a steer, rather than being hand decorated with a platinum point. This was a very popular medium for novelties and souvenirs sold at the popular resorts such as Niagra Falls, the Catskills and Coney Island. Albums for photographs, postcards and autographs were popular as well as practical novelties such as needle cases and other sewing accessories. The American Indian provided the inspiration for many of the designs. Postcards made from branded leather were a popular novelty that are still readily available from postcard dealers.

A hundred years ago this was all very new. The excitement of burning designs combined with simple wood carving and coloring was very real when compared with the more traditional pastimes of embroidery or calligraphy. The ability to produce a whole range of new things that could be used in the home, or made as gifts for loved ones, was very appealing. The popularity of pyrography even allowed some ladies to become entrepreneurs and produce gifts for sale or give lessons to the public.

The decline seems to have occurred from about 1910 onwards. The thrills provided by the bicycle, the phonograph, electric light and the motor car provided just too much competition and when America entered the First World War the ladies used their skills for more important tasks.

Today there are very few active pyrographers. It is once again a hobby for men with time on their hands.

The Manufacturers and Art Supply Companies

The original kits and supplies were normally available by mail order or through a network of general stores. The manufacture of these articles was dominated by the Flemish Art Company (FAC) in New York City and the Thayer & Chandler Company, (T&C) at 160 - 164 W. Jackson Blvd. in Chicago. Minor companies included The Solar Pyro, Mfg. Co. of New York and A.H. Balliet of Allentown, PA. Manufacturers of Pyrographic Boxes and Novelties. All these companies supplied the major mail order companies of the day including Sears in Chicago and F.F. Frick and Co. of Buffalo, New York together with many local art supply companies such as F. Weber & Co. of Chestnut Street, Philadelphia and St. Louis, Frost and Adams, of Boston and Edward Malley and Co. of New Haven.

Thayer and Chandler were major suppliers of artist's materials and were very innovative in introducing new designs. They certainly had the largest catalogue but based on the number of surviving pieces they never outsold the Flemish Art Co. In 1903 they pulled off something of a coup when they obtained copyright permission from Collier's Weekly, to reproduce Charles Dana Gibson's popular pen and ink drawings of young ladies. These "Gibson Girls" were inspired by a composite of popular actresses of the day and have been described as "fashioned for masculine adoration, but absolutely unresponsive." However, in many of the scenes in which they are being courted by a very nice young man, they do appear to be responding! The Gibson Beau was based on Richard Harding Davis, a friend who wrote many of the stories illustrated by Gibson. The "Gibson Girl" was big business. Colliers paid Gibson $100,000 for 100 sketches and while we don't know how much Thayer & Chandler paid for the reproduction rights we do know the girls appear on many products. They even adorn the legs of tables.

Another artist who had great influence on the graphic designs was Alphonse Mucha, famous for his beautiful Art Nouveau lithographs including the ones of Sarah Bernhardt. He taught for a time at the New York School of Applied Design for Women. His influence is most obvious in the products made by Thayer & Chandler who's designs were generally more fashion conscious than the more traditional heraldic approach used by the other manufacturers.

Today we tend to think that the merchandising of popular fictional characters such as Snoopy or Mickey Mouse is a modern phenomena but it was frequently used by Victorian manufacturers. Thayer and Chandler used many such graphic designs on their products. The Sunbonnet Babies were originally drawn by Bertha May Corbett as primer illustrations that show young children with large bonnets doing household chores. They also appeared on Royal Bayreuth china. The Gorman Siver Co. used a design called "Venus Awakening," which showed a sleeping lady being kissed by an angel, on a range of articles including a ladies dresser set. This same design appears in the Thayer & Chandler catalog but we have never seen a burnt example. Gibson's Girls were depicted on many products by Raphael Tuck & Sons and porcelain from the Royal Doulton Company. Corbett's Overall Boys can also be found on many Thayer and Chandler products.

Sears, Roebuck & Co. started to feature pyrography in their 1902 Fall Catalog using Thayer and Chandler products. This first venture was limited to plaques, a few photo frames, a scrap basket, three steins and a book rack. The response must have been positive because the next year they advertised a separate catalog and by 1907 a full page of the main catalog was devoted to pyrography. In the fall of 1911 Sears switched from Thayer & Chandler products to the Flemish Art Co. We do not know why they made this move from a local Chicago supplier to one situated in New York but the announcement of a new supplier infers that product quality was an issue.

The Flemish Art Company claimed to be the "World's Largest Manufacturer of Pyrographic Supplies." It is the most famous name today. They appear to be the only company that 'signed' most of their pieces and so, over the years, Flemish Art became accepted as a generic term to describe pyrography. Other manufacturers' names are less often seen on pieces and can be identified only from a study of sales catalogs. Around 1905 the Flemish Art Co. tried to respond to the popularity of the Gibson Girls by obtaining copyright permission from Moffat, Yard & Co. NY to reproduce pictures by Howard Chandler Christie. Christie was also famous for his line drawings of young ladies and his depictions of courting couples or newlyweds involved in the fashionable pursuits of the day. Sailing, playing cards, quarrelling and making up. Christie is usually acknowledged as the more famous artist and earned even more money than Gibson. His illustrations were more complex and did not easily lend themselves to interpretation by pyrography. As a result, examples are very difficult to find.

The other manufacturing companies had to develop their own imitations of these famous artists and there are many examples with "Gibson Girls" look-alikes.

Identifying Manufacturers

Depending on your approach to collecting, identifying the manufacturer of unmarked pieces can either be part of the fun or an irrelevant exercise. The simplistic approach is to assume that any unmarked piece was made by Thayer & Chandler and surprisingly you will be right more often than not. The most reliable method is to find the actual piece illustrated in one of the manufacturers' catalogs. Collecting catalogs and other pyrography related emphemera is a hobby of its own. We have included a few pages from a Thayer & Chandler catalog to whet your appetite.

THAYER & CHANDLER, CHICAGO

Three-Ply Basswood Frames for Decorating

STAMPED WITH DESIGN. FITTED WITH GLASS AND RING. OPENINGS. 5⅝ IN.

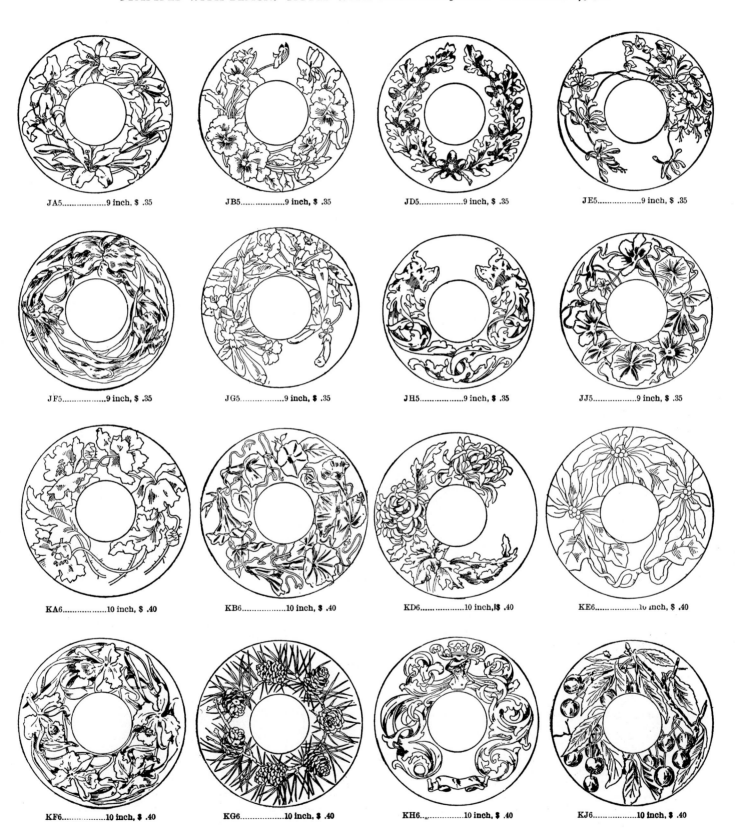

JA5......9 inch, $ .35	JB5......9 inch, $ .35	JD5......9 inch, $ .35	JE5......9 inch, $ .35
JF5......9 inch, $ .35	JG5......9 inch, $ .35	JH5......9 inch, $ .35	JJ5......9 inch, $ .35
KA6......10 inch, $ .40	KB6......10 inch, $ .40	KD6......10 inch, $ .40	KE6......10 inch, $ .40
KF6......10 inch, $ .40	KG6......10 inch, $ .40	KH6......10 inch, $ .40	KJ6......10 inch, $ .40

Decorated Frames, Pyro-etched and Hand Colored with Water Colors, each **$1.25.**

Peerless Patent Cork Handles control the heated point perfectly for steady low, medium or high temperature burning. See **page 5.**

THAYER & CHANDLER, CHICAGO

Three-Ply Basswood Frames for Decorating

FITTED WITH GLASS, BACK AND STANDARD

These copyrights fully protected. We have the exclusive right to reproduce for pyrographic decoration on wood, these pictures by
CHARLES DANA GIBSON
Beautifully colored fac-simile study furnished with each frame shown in upper row.

American College Girl Frames

Outside, 8x10. Cab. Opening.
RD47, stamped, $ .65
Including colored study.

Outside, 8x10. Cab. Opening.
RB48, stamped, $ .65
Including colored study.

Outside, 8x10. Cab. Opening.
RE49, stamped, $ .65
Including colored study.

Outside, 8x10. Cab. Opening.
RF49 stamped, $ .65
Including colored study.

Outside, 8x10. Cab. Opening.
ME47, stamped, $ .50

Outside, 11x15. Cab. Openings.
VA86, stamped, $ .85

Outside, 8x10. Cab. Opening.
MG49, stamped, $ .50

Outside 11x15. Cab. Openings.
VB86, stamped, $ .85

Outside, 8x10. Cab. Opening.
MD50, stamped, $ .50

Outside, 11x15. Cab. Openings.
VD86, stamped, $ .85

Peerless Patent Cork Handles control the gas fed to the point perfectly for steady low, medium or high temperature burning. See page 5.

THAYER & CHANDLER, CHICAGO.

BASSWOOD ARTICLES FOR DECORATING

PANEL, 18 in.
Mounted with imported fac-simile.
DMB141. Stamped $1.50
KMC141. Decorated 4.50

BEVELED MIRROR AND FRAME.
Outside 19x22, Mirror 14x17.
MAA33. Stamped $5.00
YA33. Decorated 10.00

PANEL, 18 in.
Mounted with imported fac-simile.
DME141. Stamped $1.50
KME141. Decorated 4.50

MEDICINE CABINET, 17x26½.
HMT704. Stamped $3.50
HAO704. Plain 3.00
YC704. Decorated 13.50

THREE-PLY PANELS, Stamped Border, 18x36.
Mounted with fine imported fac-simile decorative figure.
HAA236. Iris and Figure $3.00
HAB236. Roses and Figure 3.00
HAD236. Poppies and Figure 3.00
HAE236. Daisies and Figure 3.00

CHINA CABINET AND PLATE RACK. Fancy Glass.
30½x36. 6 in. deep.
SGT705. Stamped $7.25
PMO705. Plain 6.50
YC705. Decorated 24.00

BOOK STAND AND CABINET, 15¼x54¾.
SGT684. Stamped $7.25
PMO684. Plain 6.50
YC684. Decorated 24.00

TEA TABLE, 28x36, height 29 in.
MAT721. Stamped $5.00
KMO721. Plain 4.50
YC721. Decorated 22.00

MAGAZINE STAND, 13½x43.
KGV683. Stamped $4.25
HTO683. Plain 3.75
YC683. Decorated 18.00

THAYER & CHANDLER, CHICAGO.

BASSWOOD ARTICLES FOR DECORATING

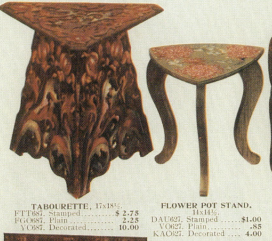

TABOURETTE, 17x18½.
FTT687. Stamped......$ 2.75
FGO687. Plain.......... 2.25
YC687. Decorated...... 10.00

FLOWER POT STAND, 14x14½.
DAU627. Stamped......$1.00
FGO627. Plain.......... .85
KAC627. Decorated.... 4.00

JARDINIERE STAND, 16x18.
FTT686. Stamped......$ 2.75
FGO686. Plain.......... 2.25
YC686. Decorated...... 10.00

FLOWER POT STAND, 12x14½.
DAU630. Stamped......$1.00
VO630. Plain.......... .85
KAC630. Decorated.... 4.00

SCRAP BASKET, 18 in.
DGA552. Stamped (knocked down)$1.25
DAX552. Plain (knocked down)...... 1.00
YC552. Decorated...... 10.00

FRUIT PANEL, 16x30.
DGB182½. Stamped......$ 1.50
YB182½. Decorated...... 10.00

FIREPLACE SCREEN, 32x38. Fitted with Reversible Hinges.
MAA703. Stamped..........................$ 5.00
KGX703. Plain............................ 4.25
YC703. Decorated......................... 25.00

UMBRELLA STAND, 10x22. Fitted with Metal Pan.
FMT688. Stamped......$ 2.50
FAO688. Plain.......... 2.00
YC688. Decorated...... 12.00

HALL CHAIR, 39 in.
FVU673. Stamped......$ 2.85
FMO673. Plain.......... 2.50
YC673. Decorated...... 12.00

COAT HANGER, 18x38.
KAA731. Stamped..........................$ 4.00
HMX731. Plain............................ 3.50
YC731. Decorated......................... 15.00

SHIRT WAIST BOX, 16x30½. Height, 16½ in.
MMT304. Stamped..........................$ 5.50
MAO304. Plain............................ 5.00
YC304. Decorated......................... 22.00

SMOKER'S CABINET, 18x45.
MAV685. Stamped......$ 5.00
KMO685. Plain.......... 4.50
YC685. Decorated...... 25.00

Holly and Basswood Novelties for Decorating

Holly Paper Knives, 10¾ in.

PA538 Stamped, $ .60   MX538 Plain, $ .50

PA539 Stamped, $ .60   MX539 Plain, $ .50

PA540 Stamped, $ .60   MX540 Plain, $ .50

Holly Paper Knives, 10¾ in.

PA541 Stamped, $ .60   MX541 Plain, $ .50

PA542 Stamped, $ .60   MX542 Plain, $ .50

MA543, 12 in., Stamped, $ .50   KX543, 12 in., Plain, $ .40

Holly Paper Knives, 9 in.

HA544 Stamped, $ .30   FX544 Plain, $ .20

HA545 Stamped, $ .30   FX545 Plain, $ .20

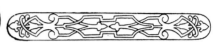
HA546 Stamped, $ .30   FX546 Plain, $ .20

Calendars

JA561, 7 in., Stamped, $ .35

Desk Clock and Calendar Stand. 7x8 in. Fitted with Standard.
DVA537 Stamped, $1.85

JA468, 7½ in., Stamped, $ .35

JB468, 7½ in., Stamped, $ .35

MB467, 8 in., Stamped, $ .50

Thermometers

MA464 Stamped, $ .50

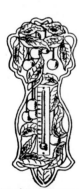
KA463, 9½ in. Stamped, $ .40

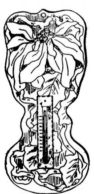
KA462, 10 in., Stmp., $ .40

Calendars

JA465, 10 in., Stmp., $ .35

JA466, 9½ in. Stmp., $ .35

JB485, 10 in. Stmp., $ .35

Pen Tray, 9¾ in.
JB519 Stamped, $ .35
GX519 Plain,   .25

Pen Tray, 9 in.
JD519 Stamped, $ .35
GX519 Plain,   .25

Blotter, 3 x 6 in., fitted with Polished Spring Brass Blotter Holder.
KA489 Stamped, $ .40   HX489 Plain, $ .30

Ink Stand, 8 in., fitted with double well.
TA490 Stamped, $ .75
PX490 Plain,   .60

Letter Rack, 5½ x 8 in.
RA573 Stamped, $ .65
MX573 Plain,   .50

Stationery Holder, 4 x 7 in.
FAA536 Stamped, $1.00
UX536 Plain,   .80

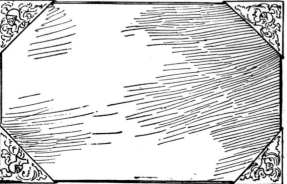
Desk Pad, 12 x 19 in.   White Wood Corners.
DMA574 Stamped, $1.50   DJK574 Plain, $1.35

Stationery Holder, 3 x 7 in.
MA535 Stamped, $ .50
KX535 Plain   .40

Stationery Holder, 3 x 7 in.
MB535 Stamped, $ .50
KX535 Plain   .40

Stationery Holder, 10 in.
TA491 Stamped, $ .75
MX491 Plain,   .50

Basswood Novelties for Decorating

Nail Brush, 3/4x6½ inches.
LA529, stamped, $ .45
KX529, plain, .40

Tooth Brush, 5/8x6½ inches.
KA528, stamped, $ .40
JX528, plain, .35

Hair Brush, 2¾x8 inches
WA532, stamped, $ .90
TX532, plain, .75

Cloth Brush, 2x6¾ inches.
DAA534, stamped, $1.00
WX534, plain, .90

Complexion Brush, 2¼x3¾ inches.
LA530, stamped, $ .45
JX530, plain, .35

Hat Brush, 1¼x5½ inches.
SA531, stamped, $ .70
PX531, plain, .60

Military Brush, 3x5 inches.
SA533, stamped, $ .70
PX533, plain, .60

Jewel Stand, 5¼ inches.
RA486, stamped, $ .65
MX486, plain, .50

Jewel Tray, 5 inches.
HA383, stamped, $ .30
GX383, plain, .25

Match Stand, 3¾ in.
KA385, stamped, $ .40
HX385, plain, .30

Hat Pin Holder, 6 inches.
With button receptacle.
PA394, stamped, $ .60
MX394, plain, .50

Hat Pin Holder, 5½ inches.
PA395, stamped, $ .60
MX395, plain, .50

Sand Glass, 3½ inches.
3 min.
JA487, stamped, $ .35
GX487, plain, .25

Burnt Match Holder.
LA397, stamped, $ .45
KX397, plain, .40

White Holly Button, 1⅜ inch.
DA389, stamped, $ .10
DX389, plain, .10

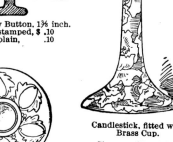
Candlestick, fitted with Brass Cup.

Size	Stamped	
10 inch,	WA365,	$ .90
12 inch,	DAA366,	1.00
16 inch,	DEA367,	1.15

Size	Plain	
10 inch,	TX365,	$ .75
12 inch,	VX366,	.85
16 inch,	WX367,	.90

Candle Stick, 8x12½ inches.
Three-Ply.
Fitted with Brass Cups.
RA497, stamped, $ .65

Candle Stick, 8x12½ inches.
Three-Ply.
Fitted with Brass Cups.
RA498, stamped, $ .65

Candlestick, 14x17½ inches,
Fitted with Brass Cups.
DGA547, stamped, $1.25

White Holly Button, 1⅝ inch.
DA388, stamped, $ .10
DX388, plain, .10

Napkin Ring.
EA387, stamped, $ .15
DX387, plain, .10

Saucer and Cover for Medicine Glass.
MA400, stamped, $ .50
(without glass)
KX400, plain, $ .40
(without glass)

Book Rack, 6½x15 inches.
Extension   Stationary
DAA505, stamped, $1.00   MA506, stamped, $ .50
WX505, plain, .90   KX506, plain, .40

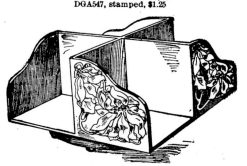
Revolving Book Stand, 12x12 inches.
FEA567, stamped, $2.15
DVX567, plain, 1.85

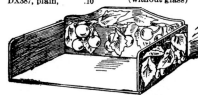
Magazine Holder, 7½x11½ inches.
DAA568, stamped, $1.00
UX568, plain, .80

Book Rack, 6½x15 inches.
Extension   Stationary
DAA499, stamped, $1.00   MA500, stamped, $ .50
WX499, plain, .90   KX500, plain, .40

Book Rack, 6½x15 inches.
Extension   Stationary
DAA501, stamped, $1.00   MA502, stamped, $ .50
WX501, plain, .90   KX502, plain, .40

Book Rack, 6½x15 inches.
Extension   Stationary
DAA503, stamped, $1.00   MA504, stamped, $ .50
WX503, plain, .90   KX504, plain, .40

BASSWOOD ARTICLES FOR DECORATING

PIN CUSHION, 6½x6½ in.
Assorted Colors.
MA800. Stamped . . **$0.50**
KX800. Plain . . . **.40**

PIN CUSHION, 6¾ in.
Assorted Colors.
PA804. Stamped . . **$0.60**
LX804. Plain . . . **.45**

PIN CUSHION, 4½ in.
Assorted Colors.
LB801. Stamped ...$0.45
KX801. Plain ...... .40

PIN CUSHION, 5x7 in.
Assorted Colors.
PA803. Stamped....$0.60
LX803. Plain........ .45

BON BON DISH.
TA360. Stamped .$0.75
NX360. Plain...... .55
FGC360. Decorated 2.25

FANCY BOXES, Stamped.

5¼x 8¼	RB292.	$0.65	8 x11	XB295.	$0.95
6 x 9	SB293.	.70	8¾x11¾	DBB296.	1.05
7 x10	VB294.	.85			

OVAL CARD TRAYS.
See page 23 for sizes and prices.

MATCH HANGER, 11 in.
LA482. Stamped..$0.45
DGA482. Decorated.1.25

VASE, 12 in.
Inside Waterproof.
FGA361. Stamped.$2.25
FAX361. Plain..... 2.00
UAC361. Decorated 8.00

MATCH HANGER
11 in.
LB482. Stamped, $0.45
DGC482. Decorated, 1.25

GLOVE BOX, 4x11½ in.
PD266. Stamped $0.60
KX266. Plain .... .40
FTC266. Decorated................. 2.75

LACE BOX, 9x12 in.
TD270. Stamped, **$0.75** NX270. Plain, **$0.55**
HMC270. Decorated, **$3.50**

SPECIAL SEWING BOX, 10½x14½ in.
DAB273. Stamped $1.00
TX273. Plain .... .75
PAC273. Decorated...................................... 6.00

HEART BOXES.

Size.	Stamped.		Plain.	
3¼x4	KB279.	$0.40	HX279.	$0.30
4½x5	LB280.	.45	JX280.	.35
5¼x6	NB281.	.55	LX281.	.45
6¼x7	RB282.	.65	MX282.	.50
7¼x7¼	TB283.	.75	PX283.	.60
8¼x8¼	VB284.	.85	SX284.	.70

HDKF. BOX, 6x6 in.
TA263. Stamped .$0.75
PX263. Plain..... .60
HAC263. Decorated 3.00

OVAL BOXES, Stamped.

3¼x6¼	LD285.	$0.45	5¼x 8¼	PD288.	$0.60
4 x7	MD286.	.50	6 x 9	SD289.	.70
4¾x7¾	ND287.	.55	6¼x 9¼	TD290.	.75
			7¼x10¼	UD291.	.80

HEART BOXES, Stamped.

3¼x4	KE279	$0.40	6¼x7	RE282	$0.65
4½x5	LE280	.45	7¼x7¼	TE283	.75
5¼x6	NE281	.55	8¼x8¼	VE284	.85

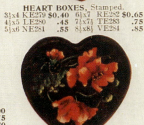

NECK TIE or STOCK BOX, 4x15 in.
TA267. Stamped....$0.75 NX267. Plain....$0.55
HMC267. Decorated....$3.50

VASE, 10 in.
Inside Waterproof.
FAA364. Stamped ..$2.00
DTX364. Plain...... 1.75
PMC364. Decorated. 6.50

OVAL BOXES, Stamped.

4 x7	MA286.	$0.50	6 x 9	SA289.	$0.70
4¾x7¾	NA287.	.55	6¼x 9¼	TA290.	.75
5¼x8¼	PA288.	.60	7¼x10¼	UA291.	.80

NECK TIE or STOCK BOX, 4x15 in.
TB267. Stamped....$0.75 NX267. Plain....$0.55
HTC267. Decorated....$3.75

CARD TRAYS, Stamped.

4½x5	GB425	$0.25	7¼x7¼	KB428	$0.40
5¼x6	HB426	.30	8¼x8¼	LB429	.45
6¼x7	JB427	.35			

COLLAR BOX, 8 in.
Fitted with button receptacle.
DEA355. Stamped.......$1.15
WX355. Plain.......... .90

TOBACCO JAR.
DGB356. Stamped ..$1.25
DAX356. Plain....... 1.00
KTC356. Decorated. 4.75

CUFF BOX, 6 in.
DJA354. Stamped ..$1.35
DDX354. Plain 1.10
KTC354. Decorated. 4.75

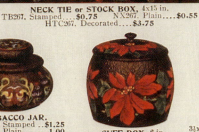

HEART BOXES, Stamped.

3¼x4	KA279.	$0.40	6¼x7	RA282.	$0.65
4½x5	LA280.	.45	7¼x7¼	TA283.	.75
5¼x6	NA281.	.55	8¼x8¼	VA284.	.85

VASE, 12 in.
Inside Waterproof.
FGA362. Stamped ..$2.25
FAX362. Plain...... 2.00
UAC362. Decorated. 8.00

SILVER TRAY, 8x12½ in.
Plush Lined.
DWA805. Stamped.................................$1.90
DRX805. Plain.. 1.65
PMC805. Decorated.................................. 6.50

HANDKERCHIEF BOX, 7x7 in.
PB265. Stamped $0.60
KX265. Plain.................... .40
HAC265. Decorated............. 3.00

VASE, 12 in.
Inside Waterproof.
FGA363. Stamped ..$2.25
FAX363. Plain...... 2.00
UAC363. Decorated. 8.00

Three-Ply Basswood Panels with Border, for Decorating
STAMPED WITH DESIGN.

Order by letter and number only. These Panels furnished with plain (unstamped) borders at the same price. If so desired, mention "Plain Border."

Size	Number	Price
9 x 12¼	JJ158	$ .35
10 x 13¾	KJ192	.40

Size	Number	Price
8½ x 12½	HE188	$ .30
13 x 18	PE196	.60

Size	Number	Price
9 x 12¼	JL158	$ .35
10 x 13¾	KL192	.40

Size	Number	Price
8½ x 12½	HG155	$ .30

Size	Number	Price
8½ x 12½	HB188	$ .30

Size	Number	Price
9 x 12¼	JK158	$ .35
10 x 13¾	KK192	.40

Size	Number	Price
8½ x 12½	HF188	$ .30

Size	Number	Price
8½ x 12½	HD188	$ .30

Size	Number	Price
8½ x 12½	HF155	$ .30
13 x 18	PF167	.60

Size	Number	Price
10 x 13¾	KK217	$ .40
13 x 18	PK196	.60

Size	Number	Price
9 x 12¼	JS158	$ .35
13 x 18	PS173	.60

Size	Number	Price
8½ x 12½	HG188	$ .30
13 x 18	PG196	.60

DECORATED PANELS. Pyro-etched and hand colored.

8½x12½ inches, $2.25   9x12¼ inches, $2.25   10x13¾ inches, $2.75   13x18 inches, $3.75

Pelican Instruction Book explains how to decorate each article for decoration listed in this catalog. Price 25 cents.

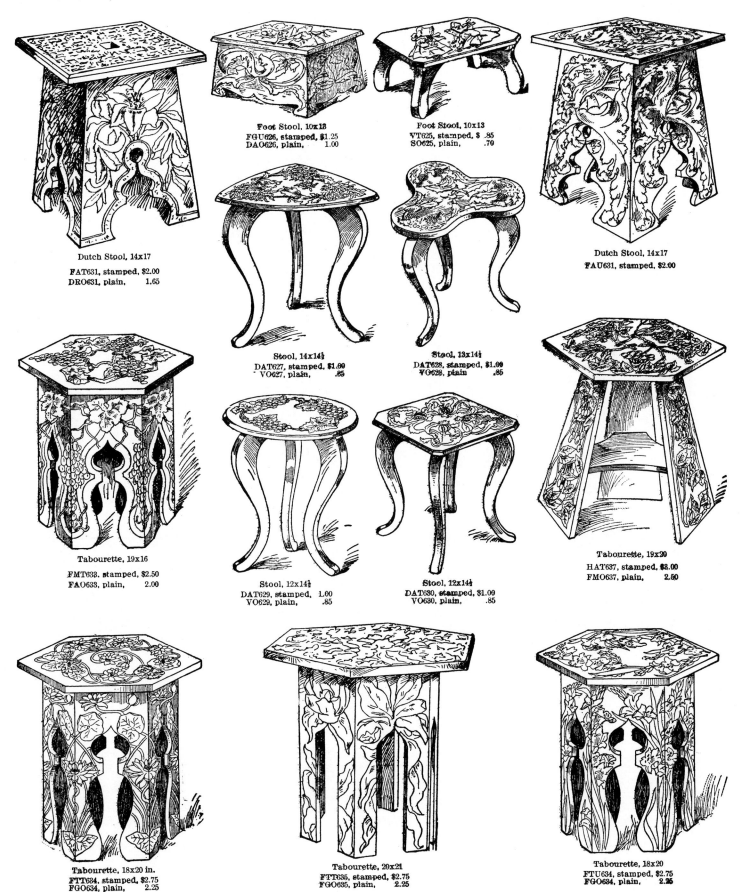

Leather Articles for Decorating

Pen Wiper, 4 inch.
FA951, stamped, $ .20
RX951, plain, .15

Pen Wiper, 4½ inch.
GA952, stamped, $ .25
FX952, plain, .20

Pen Wiper, 4 inch.
FA909, stamped, $ .20
EX909, plain, .15

Puff Box and Mirror, 2 in.
UA936, stamped, $ .80
SX936, plain, .70

Eye-Glass Cleaner.
GA935, stamped, $ .25
FX935, plain, .20

Knife Case. 3½ inch.
FA907, stamped, $ .20
EX907, plain, .15

Cigarette Case.
TA938, stamped, $ .75
RX938, plain, .65

Cigar Case.
DAA937, stamped, $1.00
VX937, plain, .85

Match Case.
JA939, st'p'd, $ .35
HA939, plain, .30

Playing Cards and Case.
VA912, st'p'd, $ .85
TX912, plain, .75

Needle and Thimble Holder, 4½ in. with Thimble.
TA942, stamped, $ .75
RX942, plain, .65

Playing Cards and Case
XA911, stamped, $ .95
VX911, plain, .85

Traveler's Roll-Up, 5x11 inch. Mackintosh Cloth Lining. Contains pockets for 1 pair Military Brushes, Cloth Brush, Shaving Stick, Tooth Brush and loops for 2 Razors.
FTA943, stamped, $2.75   FPX943, plain, $2.60

Blotter and Pen Wiper, 3½x9 inches.
MA941, stamped, $ .50   KX941, plain, $ .40

Dressing Case.
Containing Comb, Hair Brush and Tooth Brush.
FGA906, stamped, $2.25
FAX906, plain, 2.00

Laundry List, Ladies', 4x6 inches.
TA900, stamped, $ .75
RX900, plain, .65

Laundry List, Men's
TA901, stamped, $ .75
RX901, plain, .65

Collar Holder, 6 inches.
DVA945, stamped, $1.85
DTX945, plain, 1.75

Cuff Holder, 14 inches.
DRA946, stamped, $1.65
DMX946, plain, 1.50

Glove Box, 14 inch. Silk lined.
FMA910, stamped, $2.50   FGX910, plain, $2.25

Calendar Stand, 3½x4½ inches
Fitted with perpetual calendar.
TA940, stamped, $ .75 RX940, plain, $ .65

Kodak Book, 7x10 inches. 100 pages.
FGA944, stamped, $2.25
FAX944, plain, $2.00

Telephone Index, 7½x11½ inches.
FMA947, stamped, $2.50
FGX947, plain, 2.25

Pipe Holder, 11x14 inches.
DAA948, stamped, $1.00
VX948, plain, .85

Indian Hanger, 11x14 inches.
WA949, stamped, $ .90
TK949, plain, .75

Pipe Holder, 8½x12 inches.
DAA950, stamped, $1.00
VX950, plain, .85

Use Thayer & Chandler's English Oil Colors for coloring pyrographic decorations on leather.

THAYER & CHANDLER, CHICAGO

Naan Plush Cushion Covers, for Decorating

All designs listed on this page are stamped on regular size Cushion Fronts.

Empire Green, Crimson, Sapphire, Old Gold, Tan, Sage Green, Pearl Gray, Ecru, Ashes of Roses, White. Mention color desired when ordering.

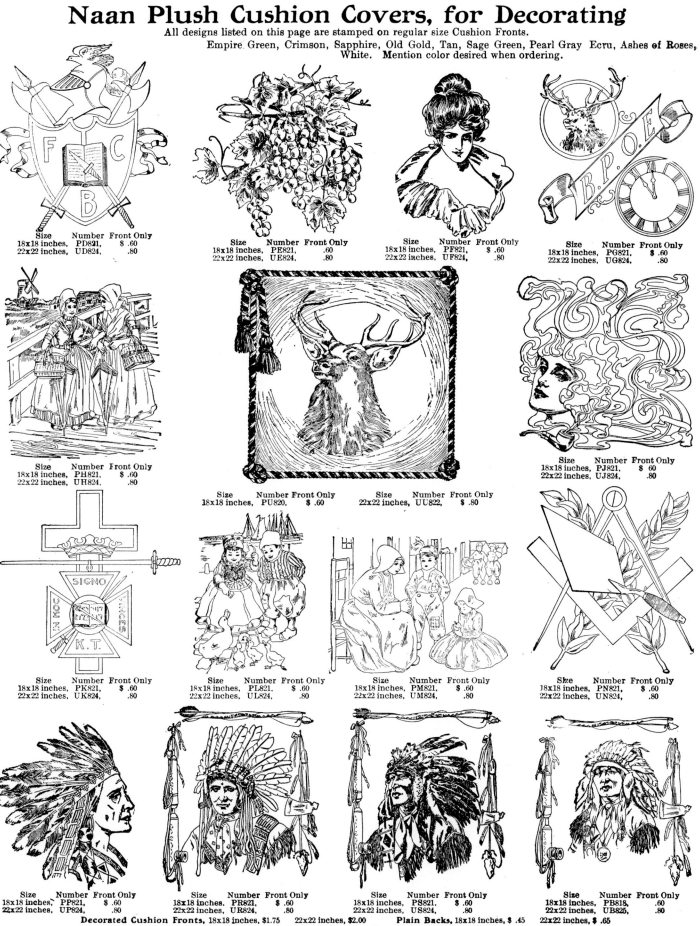

Size	Number	Front Only
18x18 inches,	PD821,	$ .60
22x22 inches,	UD824,	.80

Size	Number	Front Only
18x18 inches,	PE821,	.60
22x22 inches,	UE824,	.80

Size	Number	Front Only
18x18 inches,	PF821,	$ .60
22x22 inches,	UF824,	.80

Size	Number	Front Only
18x18 inches,	PG821,	$ .60
22x22 inches,	UG824,	.80

Size	Number	Front Only
18x18 inches,	PH821,	$ .60
22x22 inches,	UH824,	.80

Size	Number	Front Only
18x18 inches,	PU820,	$ .60

Size	Number	Front Only
22x22 inches,	UU822,	$ .80

Size	Number	Front Only
18x18 inches,	PJ821,	$ .60
22x22 inches,	UJ824,	.80

Size	Number	Front Only
18x18 inches,	PK821,	$ .60
22x22 inches,	UK824,	.80

Size	Number	Front Only
18x18 inches,	PL821,	$ .60
22x22 inches,	UL824,	.80

Size	Number	Front Only
18x18 inches,	PM821,	$ .60
22x22 inches,	UM824,	.80

Size	Number	Front Only
18x18 inches,	PN821,	$ .60
22x22 inches,	UN824,	.80

Size	Number	Front Only
18x18 inches,	PP821,	$ .60
22x22 inches,	UP824,	.80

Size	Number	Front Only
18x18 inches,	PR821,	$ .60
22x22 inches,	UR824,	.80

Size	Number	Front Only
18x18 inches,	PS821,	$ .60
22x22 inches,	US824,	.80

Size	Number	Front Only
18x18 inches,	PB818,	.60
22x22 inches,	UB825,	.80

Decorated Cushion Fronts, 18x18 inches, $1.75   22x22 inches, $2.00   **Plain Backs,** 18x18 inches, $ .45   22x22 inches, $ .65

See page 72 for Pillow Cords and Ruching.
See page 6 for Coloc Colors. These colors are specially prepared for painting on plush.

Comparison of the objects does give some indication of manufacturer. For example, Thayer and Chandler produced many more variations of picture frames than the Flemish Art Company who produced more wall thermometers and other novelty items.

With the exception of the copyrighted work of the original artists, comparison of subject matter is complicated as manufacturers often copied each other's designs. Good examples are the muzzled puppy, known at the time as "The Growl" design and the three horse heads known in fine art circles as "Pharaohs Horses." These designs appear everywhere.

Another very good indicator is the hardware used on the product. Each manufacturer of boxes seems to have favored a different design of clasp. Boxes produced by the Flemish Art Company and Thayer & Chandler inevitably have a clasp where the latch part of the clasp has bulbous ends but the smaller companies used a range of individual clasp designs.

Boxes that are marked "A.H. Balliet Allentown, Pa.," on the base often have a triangular shaped side hinge marked "WIZARD L.F. Grammes & Sons, Allentown, Pa." We have also found boxes with "WHS" stamped within the design that use these hinges. Perhaps these boxes were also made by Balliet and WHS was the designer. The same shape of hinge but stamped "Box Mfrs. PLATT-MASCHER, Chicago" have also been found. Geographic location would suggest that these boxes were distributed by Thayer and Chandler but we have no evidence of this.

We do know from studying the catalogs that the Flemish Art Company used wire standards for desk top picture frames while Thayer & Chandler used solid, hinged standards.

Surprisingly, a more reliable approach is to compare the size of the blanks and standard used by each company. This works very well for plaques, frames and boxes. It is also helpful in determining the intended use for the hundreds of different boxes that were produced. We have tabulated some of this information to help you identify Thayer & Chandler products. More research is needed to substantiate these approaches to identifying manufacturers, particularly for the smaller companies.

Box Identification By Size of Base
Table 1 - Hinged Lid Boxes

Size (inches)	Use	Man.F.	Size (inches)	Use	Man.F.
2 x 3	Stamp	FAC	5 x 31	Dresser	FAC
2 x 4$^{1/2}$	Stamp	FAC	5$^{3/4}$ x 6$^{3/8}$	Handkerchief	FAC
2$^{1/2}$ x 3$^{3/4}$	Stamp	T & C	6 x 6	Handkerchief	T & C
3 x 6	Bon Bon	Balliet	6 x 6	Collar & Cuff	FAC
3$^{1/2}$ x 4$^{1/2}$	Jewel	FAC	6 x 7/8	Work	FAC
4 x 6	Cigar	T & C	6$^{1/4}$ x 9$^{3/4}$	Cigar	T & C
4 x 6	Trinket	T & C	6$^{3/8}$ x 6$^{3/8}$	Collar & Cuff	FAC
4 x 11	Glove	T & C	6$^{1/2}$ x 9$^{3/4}$	Cigar	FAC
4 x 11$^{1/2}$	Glove	T & C			
4$^{1/4}$ x 11$^{3/4}$	Glove	FAC			
4$^{1/2}$ x 31$^{1/2}$	Dresser	T & C			
4$^{3/4}$ x 6$^{3/4}$	Jewel	T & C			

Box Identification By Size of Base
Table 2 - Lift Off Lid Boxes

Size (inches)	Use	Man.F.
2 x 3$^{5/8}$	Pin	FAC
3 x 5$^{1/2}$	Pin	FAC
3$^{1/2}$ x 4$^{1/2}$	Card	T & C
3$^{1/2}$ x 4$^{3/8}$	Card	T & C
3$^{3/4}$ x 3$^{3/4}$	Stud	FAC

Size (inches)	Use	Man.F.
3$^{3/4}$ x 4$^{3/4}$	Card	FAC
4 x 6	Jewel	T & C
4 x 6	Cigar	T & C
6 x 6	Handkerchief	T & C

Box Identification By Size of Base
Table 3 - Fancy Boxes

DIA (inches)	Use	Man.F.
2$^{5/8}$	Bon Bon	FAC
3	Cord	FAC
3$^{1/2}$	Jewel	T & C
3$^{1/2}$	Trinket	T & C
4	Trinket	T & C

DIA (inches)	Use	Man.F.
4$^{1/4}$	Trinket	T & C
5	Puff	T & C
5	Trinket	T & C
5	Bon Bon	T & C
7	Round	FAC

NOTE: Most oval, heart and serpentine shaped boxes were made by T & C, with the exception of a 5$^{7/8}$" x 6$^{1/4}$" heart shaped base made by FAC.

How to Evaluate Workmanship and Assess Value

The present market is in the developmental stage and none of the well known price guides include pyrography as a category. Although retail prices vary widely there has been a very strong trend upwards as more dealers have come to appreciate this art form. In order to purchase with confidence you will have to develop your own concept of relative value and take it from there. Obviously, if you are new to this field, recognizing rarity will be impractical but if you base your evaluation on condition and quality you will not go far wrong.

There are several reasons why now is a great time to start a pyrography collection.

* Good examples can still be found in the popular $50 to $2000 price range.

* There are plenty of pieces available in many collector categories.

* Most of the items were made between 1895 and 1915 so are about to become genuine, one hundred year old antiques.

* Collector interest in this period, covering the last few years of the Victorian era and extending into the Edwardian period remains strong.

* There are no reproductions to worry about.

The popularity of different objects obviously has a major impact on value. A plaque of a Gibson Girl playing golf is more collectible, and therefore worth more, than a pipe rack of a laughing monk, unless you collect pipe racks or images of laughing monks. Similarly, a large piece of furniture is going to be worth more than a picture frame even though more people may be able to buy and use the picture frame.

Fortunately we can all judge comparative values of two or more similar items without a vast technical knowledge. We just need to examine each piece closely and think about what we see. A few years ago we wanted to but a string of pearls while on vacation in Hawaii. With great trepidation we entered a shop and admitted to the owner that we knew nothing about pearls. He smiled and said "You know a lot about pearls" and proceeded to set out four strings with the price tags turned over. He asked "Which string do you prefer?" Yes, we picked the most expensive and then proceeded to correctly evaluate the other three. This process of comparison enabled us to buy with confidence a necklace that still gives pleasure. Examine several pieces and then rely on your 'gut' feelings to select the piece to buy. If you think about your collection; isn't it the item you didn't buy that you regret?

If the piece talks to you and you can afford it buy it!

Although there is no reproduction market, pyrography is being produced today in many parts of the world. Fortunately the styles of design are very different from those used at the turn of the century. The effort it would take to make three ply basswood forms and then reproduce the Victorian designs, particularly those that include paint decoration and carving, is a real discouragement to fakers. Pyrography will have to significantly increase in value before reproduction becomes economically feasible. Meanwhile the articles and designs used by the major factories are well documented, thanks to the mail order catalogs. This makes establishing a basic provenance easy and reliable for any example purchased before the curse of reproductions becomes a problem.

It is very easy to recognize factory blanks with only the design printed on them. The printing is usually black, brown or purple and looks very similar to embroidery or hooked rug patterns. The major manufacturers tended to use purple or brown as they claimed these colors made the lines easier to follow. Instructions on which areas to carve or where to place jewels are often found within the areas intended to be worked. Generally speaking these have no collector value. The nearest equivalent to Faux pearls are the articles that were produced by the factories with a stamped or embossed design. The evenness of the coloration and the shallow, consistent depth of the lines makes them easy to distinguish from a piece which has also been burned. The best way for a novice to learn to identify this form of decoration is to find a box with the same design on both the inside and outside of the lid. These designs were inevitably produced by printing and embossing but most pyrographers only burned the outside of the lid. Embossed work is strictly speaking not pyrography but interesting examples are included in most collections as the manufactures sold the stamped or embossed pieces with the intention that they be burned, painted or both. As with printed boxes, stamped, or embossed wooden boxes were also used to package many consumer items from chocolates to suspenders and these are becoming very collectible.

Most Victorian pyrography was produced by overburning a factory inked design printed onto a factory made object. The quality of the point work and the wide range of the various "brush strokes" produced by different points, temperatures and speeds, is what makes this pyrography special. The artists use of these factors is a paramount importance in transforming the factory produced designs into true works of art. The outlines should be fluid and unbroken and the background shadings must add detail or provide impact. It is often the quality of the background work that makes the piece come alive. While the types of lines, shadings and background designs used are infinite, we have illustrated the most common ones to help you when assessing or describing an example. (shown on next page.)

When burning covers the entire background we have what was traditionally known as all over burning but today this is frequently identified as pyromania. In many cases it does appear as if the artist could not stop until every surface was covered with intricate burn marks. This approach may apply to factory designs or be entirely the result of the pyrographers running wild with their imagination. These pieces are usually very bold, dramatic, and inevitably expensive.

Historically, painting was often combined with pyrography and is certainly a major feature of Victorian pyrography. Good painting brings out the detail and adds another dimension to the work but a daubed piece can ruin good burn work. Most pieces were painted by the individual pyrographers but the manufacturers also supplied furniture and other articles that had been burned and painted in the factory. It's interesting that while the instruction manuals encouraged the artist to use water colors, "To allow the beauty of the wood to show through," the manufacturers tended to use the more opaque oil paints on their products. The relatively high cost of the factory painted pieces prevented many people from purchasing them and furthermore pyrography was supposed to be a do it yourself hobby for the emerging middle class. This was instant pyrography for the idle rich, but as very few pieces exist, they attract premium prices.

As with all antiques condition is an important factor in determining value. The highest value applies to pieces that are in mint condition, with original finish and proven provenance. Very few such pieces have survived. Furniture usually shows signs of wear, and the occasional ding from nearly 100 years of wear and minor repair on an easy to find small box will make the piece unworthy of collecting.

The best advice we can give you when you buy is to go for quality not quantity. Yes you will occasionally get a real steal but beware, more often than not the cheap piece is no bargain. Don't buy on price alone. It's the last factor you should consider. Reject more pieces than you buy.

Backgrounds

PEPPER
   The easiest background to produce. Made with the extreme end of the point and low heat.

DOT
   Produced with a blunt point at high heat. Used on large borders and furniture.

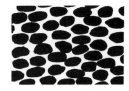

ROUGH & READY
   Long, irregular broken lines with a curved point at medium heat. Simple and effective treatment for novelty items.

WAVE
   Curved point with medium heat and a continuous motion. More difficult than it looks.

KNURLED
   Curved point at medium heat produces an effective dark background. Also used as a band on bowls or handles that need to be gripped.

PLAIN BASKET WEAVE
   Produced with sharp end of curved point. Light or heavy stroke depending on the effect required.

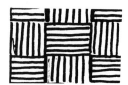

COFFEE GROUND
   Same as pepper but the dots are much closer together to give an allover effect.

DASH
   Produced with a curved point and high heat. A slow deep burn or repeated strokes produces a carved effect.

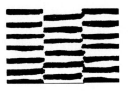

STRAIGHT LINE SHADED
   Curved point and low heat. Shading is produced by starting slow and heavy and speeding up with a lighter stroke.

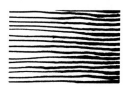

ZIG ZAG
   Curved point moved lightly over the surface. Larger version popular as a border decoration.

OAK
   Point at medium heat but working cooler and faster for lighter areas. A late development used to give a framed effect for carved pieces.

FANCY BASKET WEAVE
   Curved point at medium heat. A very popular "quality" background.

Care and Repair

Time affects the best of us and even a 'Gibson Girl" is likely to need a little tender loving care after ninety years. Unless you are fortunate enough to find a piece that has been stored away from sunlight, children and the effects of the changing seasons it's likely that it will benefit from a little loving attention.

Pieces that are in good condition may need only a light cleaning with Murphy's Oil Soap or mineral spirits, to gently remove decades of grime, followed by a light application of a good quality paste wax and a final polish with a soft cloth. We have found that an amber colored wax gives a more pleasing result than a white wax.

Many pieces were originally finished with shellac which may have become alligatored by changes in temperature and humidity. We have been successful in softening and reamalgamating the finish by gently wiping with a cloth pad moistened with a mixture of three parts denatured alcohol and one part varnish thinner. If the finish has darkened, due to years of exposure to sunlight, a heavier application will be needed to remove the shellac down to the original wood. If the finish is varnished you will need to use only varnish thinner. Follow the manufacturers directions to reshellac or varnish. Rub lightly with dry 0000 steel wool and then polish. *Never* use polyurethane as it does not allow the wood to 'breathe' and it looks too plastic on an antique. A word of caution, refinishing pyrography is tricky and time consuming. You should not attempt it unless you have some refinishing experience and a lot of patience. If you ever bought a print but never got around to matting and framing it then do not buy pieces that need work.

If the finish on a painted piece needs cleaning or restoring the work becomes even more time consuming and sometimes, frustrating. Try cleaning with Murphy's Oil Soap or mineral spirit first and see if you can live with the result.

When you have to restore or remove the shellac or varnish finish on a painted piece work very cautiously. You do not want to clean or remove the finish right down to the paint as you may remove the paint or make it bleed. Attempts to retouch the paint should be avoided. This may be done by a professional art restorer but is rarely worth the effort and expense. If you are at all worried it is advisable to restrict your activity to cleaning and polishing. This will at least maintain the integrity and value of your collection.

A final word on painted pieces. *Never, ever* buy a piece that has been badly painted or sprayed 'decorator gold.' You will never be able to remove the paint without destroying the pyrography.

It is often better to live with minor blemishes than try to make improvements. However, if you were able to clean your pieces satisfactorily you should be able to make the following repairs. Usually it is better to do the repairs before cleaning and always before polishing.

Separation of the layers of plywood is a fairly common problem but fortunately easy to fix. Gently pry the plies apart with a flat screwdriver and squeeze a good woodworking glue into the gap. Spread the glue as evenly as possible with a thin nail or a sliver of wood. A toothpick works well. Squeeze the plies together by hand and remove the excess glue as it oozes out so as not to leave marks on the edge of the wood. Clamp the plies together using two thin pieces of wood to protect the workpiece from being dented by the jaws of the clamp. If the delaminated area is large use several clamps and make sure the protective pieces of wood are large enough to help distribute the pressure over the entire area to be rejoined. For small areas we have found heavy duty "Bulldog" paper clamps work well as a substitute for woodworker's clamps.

If a joint is unglued on a small box, letter holder or similar item please do not use a nail to join it together. Not only is this repair unsightly you risk further damage by splitting the wood. A much stronger repair will be achieved if you pull the joint apart just enough to remove any old glue and to squeeze in a small amount of woodworking glue. Spread the glue, wipe off excess and clamp as before. If you don't have a suitable clamp, a couple of thick elastic bands stretched around the circumference may do the trick. Check to see that the bands hold the pieces together properly before you apply the glue.

Loose hinges can usually be fixed by removing the screws or pins then filling the holes with slivers of wood covered with a thin layer of glue. Then reinsert the screws or pins. Do not try to replace loose or missing screws with a larger size of screw. The hinge will not close properly and the wood may split.

With the exception of hinges, replacing missing or broken parts can present a real problem. Other pieces of pyrography are the only source we know for spare parts. It is possible to buy new brass catches for small boxes but the replacement will be obvious.

Pieces and Prices

Now to the Price Guide which is just what is says, a Guide. It's not written in stone but represents our interpretation of current values. By the time you read this book the values may have changed but you will still be able to use the guide to establish comparative values.

The value will generally increase depending on the number of processes used. A piece that is just printed or embossed will have only token value. It's the pyrography, carving and painting, or any combination of these processes, that provides the artistry and value. Each process should add to our appreciation of the piece and the quality of each treatment will affect the value. For example, beautiful pyro etching may be ruined by unsympathetic painting.

Personal taste obviously is very important. We like and tend to collect painted pieces but the most important factor is the quality of the pyrography. Remember, once someone started work on a factory purchased item it immediately became an individual, one of a kind piece just like a carving or painting. The only real criteria for value is how much you like it and are willing to buy or sell it for.

May we just make a plea on behalf of our fellow dealers? If you are lucky enough to find a great piece for a song at a yard sale be happy, by all means brag about it to your friends but please spare the next dealer you meet. Don't repeat your war story with the expectation of getting another piece for a similar price. Dealers love to find collectors who are willing and able to share their knowledge. These are the people who inevitably get the best buys. But "I only paid" stories are boring.

We strongly believe that in spite of recent increases, pyrography remains undervalued. More importantly, we hope that as you view the photographs you will be encouraged to enjoy and collect this aspect of American folk art.

Furniture and Major Pieces

1) This chair is exquisite. It is so finely burned that on first sight it appears to be inlaid with silky woods. The piece is hand burned all over. Very few furniture pieces include turned parts as the furniture was designed to use boards cut to shape. The furniture was shipped flat for assembly at home after burning. That's why the burned design sometimes extends through the joints. $1,000

2) Combination chair and table with very pleasing lines. When the chair back is pulled over to form a table there is velvet to the center and a burned and painted border. Lovely workmanship, probably Flemish Art. $950

3) Extremely pretty chair, very finely and delicately burned, dainty coloring. It has been hand burned and painted all over including the back. Probably Flemish Art Co. $550

4) Nicely burned plant table with Monk taking a drink but only desirable if you like Monk stuff. Quite easy to find. $180

5) Beautifully burned all over six sided stand with great detail to roses, not painted, 21" H x 13¾" W $285.

1

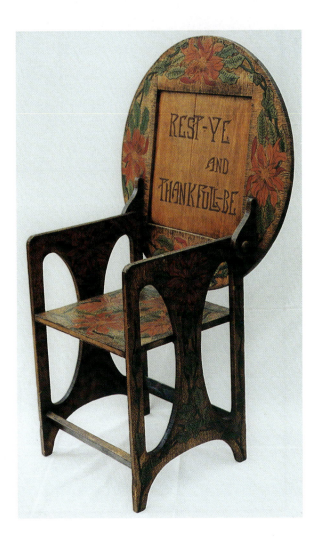

2

3

4

5

6) Pretty little sewing stand cum side table with a lift top, nicely burned, not painted. 20 1/2" H x 13 1/4" W.
$300

7) Eight sided plant stand, burnt all over, nice holly design, pretty legs. 14 1/2" H x 13" W. $295

8) Small six sided plant stand, nicely burned all over and well painted with pretty legs. 14" H x 10 1/2" W.
$300

9) Six sided stand, nicely burned with good color to poinsettias and leaves. 21" H x 15" W. $365

10) Six sided stand, absolutely beautifully burned all over and painted. They don't come in much better condition than this! 17" H x 11 3/4" W.
$400

6

7

8

9

10

11) Pure folk art two tier stand. Designed, made, hand burned and hand painted by the pyrographer most likely. Fashions and flowers adorn the legs with two female heads on the flat surfaces, probably family members. 20$^{1/2}$" H x 9$^{3/4}$" W. Hard to find piece. $465

12) Another true folk art piece. Triangular occasional table with a hand beaten copper plate in center, hand burned and painted griffins, serpents and snake creatures all over, with seashells around the edge. One stretcher is missing but this is an outstanding example of pyromania. 21$^{1/2}$" H x 21$^{1/4}$" W. $675

13) Good example of a scrap basket, beautifully hand burned, carved and painted with original leather laces. Probably Thayer and Chandler. 18" H x 10" W. $300

14) Umbrella stand fitted with metal pan, exceptional pyrography all over and fine coloring. Probably Thayer and Chandler. $365

15) Folk art smoking and drinks stand with a tiny cupboard in the center stem. This did not come from any catalog but from the imagination of the artist. Nicely burned and painted, an adorable piece that makes you smile when you look at it. Extremely hard to find this type of piece. $650

11

12

13

14

15

16) Folk art free standing or wall shelf, hand burned and painted, charming but not in the same class as the previous piece. 18" H x 13" W. $165

17) Hand burned and painted plate and cup rack with six brass hooks, nicely worked. Flemish Art Co. #844. 26 5/8" W x 10" H. $245

18) Beautiful example of a deeply burned high wall shelf., Photographed from underneath to show the sweep of the design. $325

19) Folk art clock holder. Designed, hand burned and painted by the artist. It is hand worked all over with autumnal leaves, elk, flowers and on the reverse side a small girl in clogs. A charming whimsical piece. Hard to find. $380

16

17

18

19

20) Pretty dome top chest on tiny bun feet. Very gently burned and colored with lovely lines.
    19¾" W x 13" D x 13½" H $385

21) Lovely panelled clothes chest, nicely burned and painted. Inside on the lid is burned CORNELIA H.
    BATEMAN JUNE 1904. Hard to find piece. 29" W x 16¼" D x 17½" H. $560

22) Hand burned and painted lamp base. Woman with flowing hair, stylized flowers and bands. Photograph
    does not do this justice. $350

20

21

22

Things That Should or Could Be Hung

23) Towel rack, a great example of pure pyrography. 23 1/8" L x 9" H $235

24) Magnificent folk art hand burned cue holder. Again you will not find this in any catalog. Fabulous one of a kind item. 21 1/2" W x 12" H. $650

23

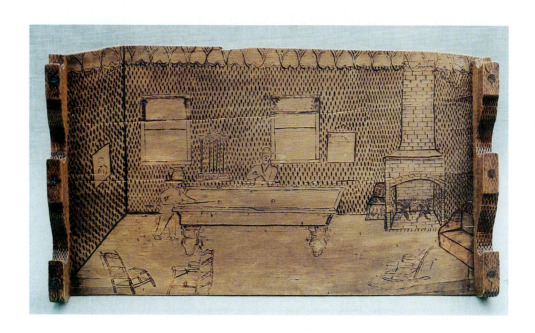

25

25) "LIZZI BORDEN" knife rack. A great piece of folk art pyrography designed and executed (excuse the pun) by the artist. You remember the Sunday School teacher from Fall River, MA who on Aug. 4, 1892 was accused of murder:

> "Lizzie Borden took an axe
> And gave her mother 40 whacks
> And when she saw what she had done
> She gave her father 41."

The general public thought she was guilty but Lizzie was acquitted of the murders in 1893. Who says history doesn't repeat itself? $550

26) Another fine example of folk art pyrography, a bread board with a sweeping design of a young boy carrying a tray of fruits. A lovely romantic feel to this piece. $450

27) A fabulous folk art piece of F.D.R. Good shading to the burning with a wonderful tree bark surround. It's another one of a kind item. $385

28) Crescent wall shelf nicely burned with good contrast. 12" H. $80

29) Beautiful hand burned panel after the painting "TO THE FEAST." The shading of the burn work is exquisite and the minimal use of gold paint to highlight is inspired. 34" W x 9½" H. $500

25

26

28

27

29

50

30) A later folk art piece. Possibly a remembrance maybe of a vaction, nicely burned and painted. A fun picture.
$200

31) "ARREST IN MUNICH" is the title of this piece, a lovely panel both in burning and painting. 20" W x 14" H.
$295

32) Folk art hand burned 7½" Dia. tray probably of the family dog. Lovely work on the back burned in H.H.D. Buck 1909, Dad 1909, Titus 1909, Pat 1909, Lenons 1907, also the following:

> May we ever stick together
> Resolved that we are and of a
> right ought to be free and
> independent characters
> of Looneyville
>   Amen

We advise you always to look at the back of a piece of pyrography. Sometimes it is as interesting as the front.
$135

33) Another example of the back being fascinating, a charming folk art piece, nicely burned and painted. On the reverse the whole family got in on the act with initials, doodles and the date 1909. 9¾" Dia. $85

34) The backs of the preceding two items.

30

31

32

33

34

52

35) Folk art burnt wood plaque, nice sentiment. 9½" x 6½" $50

36) Beautifully burned and boldly painted as befits a proud Chief. Flemish Art Co. #953, 20½" H x 9¼" W.
    $200

37) Delicately burned and softly painted as befits a lovely maiden. Flemish Art Co. #882. $185

38) Finely burned with great detail to the headdress of this 'WESTERN SON,' subtle painting and a simple, but effective burned edge. 12" Dia. $120

39) 3 ply panel carving process is used to wonderful effect on this piece to create a dramatic background for the profile of a young woman and is enhanced by the paint. Flemish Art Co. #860, 17½" x 12¼"
    $185

35

36

37

38

39

40) Gibson Girl, copyright Collier's Weekly, nicely burned and painted, Thayer and Chandler, 24½" H x 15½" W. $170

41) Left: 3 ply panel carving process used for background well burned and painted. Flemish Art. Co. #859, 11½" H x 6¾" W. $80
Center: Small 3 ply carved, burned, bejewelled, beribboned, painted and hooked. Boy does this gal have it all or what? Flemish Art Co. #361, 8" H x 3¾" W. $60
Right: Well burned and painted Florentine Panel with the work instructions on the back (shown in next photograph). Thayer & Chandler 9⅝" H x 7⅝" W. $75

42) Instructions for Florentine Panel.

43) Finely burned and boldly painted pair of 'avante guarde' female golfers, very nice, Thayer & Chandler LH 984 series. 13½" H x 10" W. $375 pair

44) Pyro etched and painted intrepid young lady fencer with nice scorched border pattern. 21" H x 7½" W. $185

40

41

44

43

42

45) Top: 3 ply carved background with nice burning and paint and 4 hooks for ribbons. Flemish Art Co. #851, 8" Dia. $70
    Bottom: Flemish Art Co. #851 again, but with very different treatment that gives impact to the college girl. $70

46) Left: Nice heart shape and very good burning to this college girl and background to give a semi relief effect. 10" H x 9⁷/₈" W. $75
    Right: Good delicate burning and painting. It may be small but this college girl is dressed to kill. Flemish Art Co. #856, 8" x 3¹/₄" W. $60

47) Subtle burning for this sailing ship and nice painting. Paper label on back reads G. FOX & CO. INC. $120

48) Fine burning for this 'NOT ANOTHER DROP' panel and it doesn't need another burn line. Flemish Art Co. #880, 20" W x 16" H. $150

45

46

47

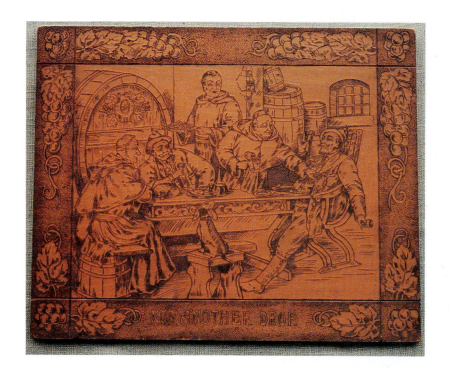

48

49) The relief burning behind this 'King of Beasts' makes the piece, light paint work. Flemish Art Co. #558 or #858, 11$^{3/4}$" Dia. $70

50) Cute as a button and not much bigger, birds and a nest full of eggs. Background is relief burned not 3 ply carved. It is also painted, only 5$^{1/2}$" Dia. Flemish Art Co. $65

51) A fishy catch, subtle burning and painting, nice. Flemish Art Co. #854, 14$^{5/8}$" Dia. $120

52) Left: A handsome pair of hounds, lovely gentle burning and paint work, on the back MERRY XMAS TO DYER, Flemish Art Co. #846, 13$^{5/8}$". $120
Right: Beautiful burning work and contrast. Just wish we could get more enthused over the subject matter! Flemish Art Co. #953 20$^{5/8}$" H x 9$^{1/4}$" W. $120

53) 'THE GROWL' 3 ply relief carved and burnt. A tiny treasure 7$^{3/8}$" Dia. Flemish Art Co. #851. $75

54) 'THE GROWL' It's that dog again, nicely burned and painted. A bigger treasure, 19$^{1/2}$" H x 13$^{1/4}$" W. $165

49

50

51

52

53

54

55) A pretty pair of panels with good all over burning and delicate painting to the Irises and daffodils. Both 10½" H x 8½" W. $60 each

56) Nicely burned and painted round plaque with the best example of basket weave burning we have seen. 12" Dia. $85

57) 3 ply carved, burned and painted round plaque. Could just pick a strawberry off, 8" Dia. $70

58) Left: Standing frame nicely burned and painted 7½" H x 6" W. $85
    Right: Standing Frame, lovely, burned and painted, Thayer & Chandler, 10" H x 8" W. $125

55

56

57

58

59) Left: Round standing frame burned and painted, very pretty, Thayer & Chandler, 9" Dia. $95
    Right: Rectangular standing frame burned and painted, boldly beautiful. 10" H x 8" W. $95

60) Standing shaped rectangular burned and painted frame with pretty bevelled round mirror to center exquisite.
    $9^{3/4}$" H x $9^{1/2}$" W. $150

61) Standing frame nice burning and painting of Oak leaves and acorns. Thayer & Chandler, $9^{3/4}$" H x 8" W.
    $125

62) Standing frame, unusual shape, nicely worked and colored. $9^{1/2}$" H x $7^{3/4}$" W. $100

63) Left: Hanging oval frame with good burning and painting. $9^{3/8}$" H x $6^{3/8}$" W. $125
    Right: Round frame nicely burned and painted, Thayer & Chandler, 7" Dia. $85

59

60

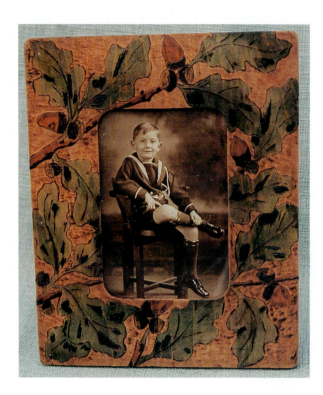

61

62

63

64) Left: Hanging round frame with a nice garland of flowers. Thayer & Chandler, 8" Dia. $85
    Right: Hanging oval frame well burned and multicolored flowers. Thayer & Chandler, 10" H x 7⅞" W.
    $125

65) Left: 3 ply carved, burned and painted rectangular frame. 10" H x 8" W. $95
    Right: Burned and painted rectangular frame 10" H x 8" W. $95

66) 3 ply carved, burned and painted small hanging mirror, very attractive, 12" H x 9" W. $140

67) Rectangular hanging frame nice burning and painting. 10½" H x 8¼" W. $125

68) Nicely burned all over pattern and well painted rectangular frame with double oval openings. 10" H x 14" W. $165

64

65

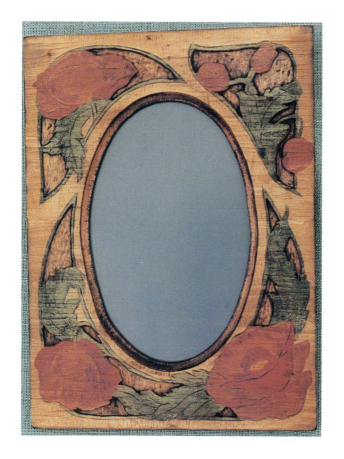

66

67

68

69) A fine example of a triple frame all hand burned with lovely contrast. Lovely prints which are original to the frame. They don't come any better than this. 16" H x 33" W. $365

70) This pair of frames have a definite folk art look with their cat tails and garlands, nicely burned and painted with a lovely autumnal feel to them. The pictures are published by Ullman Manufacturing Co., NY and are copyrighted 1901 and are original to the frames. $400 pair

71) Beautifully burned and painted triple hole rectangular frame with three fashion prints, 9" H x 17½" W. $195

72) 3 ply carved, burned and painted rectangular frame. Again a nice fall/winter feel to it which is enhanced by the winter scene which is again original to the frame. 10¾" H x 13" W. $165

73) Man's tie rack, nicely burned, good detail on the owls, some minor damage. Flemish Art Co. #441, 14" W x 10" H. $160

69

70

71

72

73

74) Ribbon rack, lovely burning and fine painting. Flemish Art Co. #508, 14" W x 6⁵⁄₈" H. $140

75) Man's tie rack. This is factory stamped but hand painted and we just love the sentiment of this one. 11¹⁄₈" W x 6⁷⁄₈" H. $125

76) Ribbon or tie rack for a lady, again stamped but hand painted and is delightful, 1" W x 6¹⁄₂" H. $125

77) His and Hers tie rack? Stamped but hand painted. This one of course is our favorite! 11" x 6¹⁄₂" H. $125

78) Child ribbon rack, stamped but hand painted, just charming, 11" W x 6¹⁄₂" H. $125

74

75

76

77

78

79) Baby's ribbon holder burning and painting of the Sunbonnet babies picking flowers. 12" W x 5 1/8" H.
$160

80) Fraternal tie rack stamped but hand painted emblems, 10 1/2" W x 6" H. $125

79

80

Smoking and Drinking

81) UNCLE SAM match holder good burning and painting. We think he is wonderful. 13" H x 7" W.
$185

82) Three novelty match holders each one is hand burned and painted and all are cute.
Top left: 5¾" H x 4" W. $95
Bottom left: THE GROWL, 4" H x 5½" W. $125
Right: 7" H x 4" W (1907 burned on back). $95

81

82

83) Lovely round covered tobacco jar hand burned with good contrast. Flemish Art Co. #61. $160

84) Beautiful smoking set, hand burned all over and nicely painted, 10" Dia. $295

85) Folk art pipe rack designed and burned by the artist. Burned on back N.D.H. L 906 SEPT., 11" W x 5" x H reads: $185
>   Beefsteak when I'm hungry
>   Whiskey when I'm dry,
>   A pretty girl when I want her
>   And heaven when I die.

86) Hand burned and painted pipe rack - Sweet dreams or impure thoughts? Flemish Art Co. #650, 8 1/2" W x 6 1/8" H. $145

83

84

85

86

87) Hand burned and painted pipe rack. This man is not having as much fun as the one in the last rack. Flemish Art Co. #650, 8 1/2" W x 6 1/8" H. $130

88) Stamped but hand painted pipe rack with lovely restful hearthside, 9 3/4" W x 8" H. $100

89) Steins were put out by both Thayer & Chandler and the Flemish Art Co.
Left: Small covered stein, well burned and painted, 6 1/8" tall + knob. $135
Right: Now this is a stein for happy hour. Nicely burned but not painted, German saying around, 23" tall. On the bottom is a partial paper label McHENRYS ………………EUCLID AVE. $295

90) Left: Folk art pyrography pitcher hollowed from one piece of wood. Handle is applied and made from a twig. 8 1/8" tall. $185
Right: Burned and painted mug with handle depicting grapes and leaves. Thayer & Chandler, 7 1/8" tall. $125

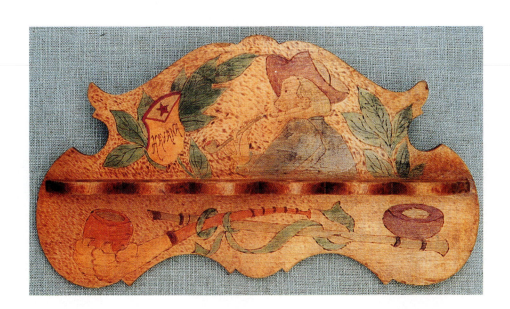

87

88

89

90

Games People Play

91) Four excellent examples of playing card boxes, all burned, painted and in lovely condition.
 Top left: Double card box with Indian maiden on the top, on the underside a teepee on a plain with mountains to back. Written on one drawer is F.R. TENBROECK, 2¼" D x 3½" W x 4" L. $145
 Bottom left: Holly design, lid lifts off. 1¼" D x 3½" W x 4" L. $95
 Top right: Hand with 4 aces, inside drawer is burned BL 1908 and underside of the drawer in pencil Virginia Edwards, Quarryville, Pennsylvania. Probably Flemish Art Co. 1½" D x 3½" W x 4" L.
     $95
 Bottom right: Good luck and armor. 1½" D x 3½" W x 4" L. $80

92) Game board all hand burned and painted both sides and edges. Open 15" square, closed 15" x 7½". Flemish Art Company. $185

93) This is a later board but it is exquisite. Made in Poland but we included it so that you can see the difference from the American style. The chessboard folds to form a box to hold the chess set. Closed 13½" x 6¾". Open 13½" square. $295

91

92

93

For the Office?

94) Deeply burned and nicely picked out with paint 1909 calendar plaque. 9" W x 5¾" H. $95

95) Charming round calendar for 1912, deep burning and nice paint for this sweet little kitty, 5¾" Dia. $50

96) Top: Hand burned and painted letter opener in shape of an oar pretty Tulip design. 9" L $50
    Bottom: This time in the shape of a spear. Again nicely worked with yellow and orange Daffodil design, 8" L. $50

97) Desk box with pen rest. The interior is sectioned. Lovely burning with good contrast. Inscribed "From Sarah Xmas 1909" and marked Flemish Art Co. #584, 8¼" L x 6" D $165

98) Four examples of stationery holders:
    Top left: Burned all around with pretty colored flowers and leaves, 8" L x 4" D x 3¾" H on underneath, "F.B. Mfg. Co. S 1249" $95
    Bottom left: Burned all around with blue flowers and leaves, 8" L x 3¾" D. $95
    Top right: Burned all around with orange daisies and leaves, 8" L x 3¾" x 3⅛" H, Flemish Art Co. #607. $95
    Bottom right: Nice all over burning with grapes and leaves finely burned and painted 7⅞" L x 3½" D x 3⅛" H. $95

94

95

96

97

98

99) Left: A later stationery rack, this time stamped but hand painted showing a sailing ship, horse pulling carriage and a steam train pulling carriage 6" L x 3 1/4" H x 3 5/8" D. $55
Right: Nicely burned stationery card holder, not painted. 5 3/4" H x 2" D x 5 1/2" W. $65

100) Top: Burned and painted pen tray very nicely done, better than the photograph shows. 9 1/2" W x 3 1/4" D. $60
Bottom: Burned and painted flowers and leaves covered pot, 3" Dia. $50

101) Three tier wall letter rack, all hand burned, absolutely beautifully, 11 1/8" H x 7" W, probably Thayer & Chandler. $185

102) Top: Burned and painted extending bookrack, nicely done. 5 5/8" W x 15 5/8" closed or 5 5/8" W x 25 1/2" extended. $125
Bottom: Burned and painted bookrack with roses on ends and in the middle, lovely, 5 3/8" W x 14" L, Flemish Art Co., #618. $145

103) Top: Shaped ends to this bookrack with lovely burning and painting all over. Stamped on bottom MA 559 T. & C. Chicago. $145
Bottom: Extending bookrack burned all over with lovely painted flowers to the ends and the middle. 5 5/8" W x 15 5/8" L closed, or 25 1/8" extended. Flemish Art Co. #623. $155

99

100

101

102

103

104) Top: Burned and painted bookrack with grapes and leaves to the ends and the middle, lovely work, 5½" W x 14" L, ink stamp on bottom C.N. Co. 818. $145

Bottom: Miss Muffet? A horrid little boy and spider (forgive us but we are a bit rusty on nursery rhymes) design on ends and to the middle of this hand burned and painted bookrack, charming piece. 5⅝" W x 14" L, stamped on bottom 818. $155

105) Top: Wise owls adorn this bookrack with good burning and painting, nice unusual piece. 6" W x 15" L. $145

Bottom: Shaped ends on this one with lovely burned designs and paint. Around the base is burned:
   Old books to read
   Old friends to trust
6" W x 15½" L. $125

106) Extending bookrack with nicely burned ends and beautifully painted girls, around the base is burned and painted:
   So long as books shall live
   There is no past.
5¾" W x 15¾" L closed and 25¼" extended. $150

107) This shows edge detail to two bookracks.

104

105

106

107

To Adorn Your Table and Impress Guests

108) Left: Nut bowl with poinsettias inside and spilling over the edge to decorate the outside, lovely burning and color. 7¾" Dia. x 2½" D. $70
Center: Autumn leaves inside and out, we think this might have been a salad bowl from wear in the middle. Burned on the underside is C.G. 3.5 D/R, a later piece 12¼" Dia. x 3½" D. $70
Right: Burned and painted with grapes and leaves inside and stylized leaves out on 4 mini bun feet, lovely. 7¾" Dia. x 2¼" D. $70

109) Left: Hand burned and painted with adorable squirrel on branch to the inside of this nut bowl. 4⅞" Dia x 1½" H. Flemish Art Co. #816. $65
Center: This nut bowl is not painted but the burning is beautiful. On the side you can't see, a squirrel is on a branch chewing a nut. The saying which is burned in says:
"When wintry winds blow fierce and cold
let nuts be cracked and stories told"
6¼" Dia x 3" H, Flemish Art Co. #723U. $75
Right: Hand burned and painted with squirrel on branch to center, charming piece. Burned on the under side NUTS Merry Xmas 1911. 7¾" Dia. x 1¾" H. $70

110) A selection of trays, each is hand burned and painted
Top left: Shaped tray with grapes and leaves 12⅝" L x 8½" D, stamped on bottom Flemish Art Co. #1071. $100
Bottom left: Tray with shaped sides "Daily Bread." May be a later piece. We have also seen it in green. 11⅝" L x 5⅞" D. $60
Right: Tray with handles, 11⅝" L x 7⅜" D. $125

111) Lovely serving tray with design and burning, not painted. $285

108

109

110

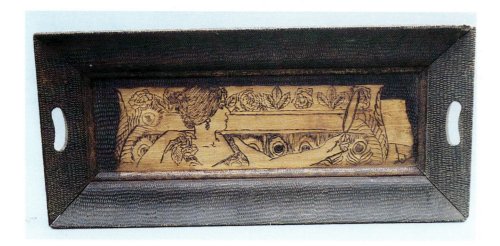

111

112) Serving fork and spoon, hand burned and painted. $60
Pair of egg cups, hand burned and painted. $60

113) Round covered container, probably for tea or coffee, hand burned and incredibly nicely painted, 7" H + the knob 5" Dia. $125

114) Left: Thread holder. These are very fragile as the wood is very thin and over the years most of them have been destroyed by harsh use. The burning had to be very carefully done or the wood would have been burned through. A pretty piece with nice painting to the top. 3" Dia. $85
Right: Lovely double hinged top sewing box with pretty center handle lovely, design, burning and painting. 9 1/2" L x 6 1/2" W. $185

115) Left: Factory stamped but hand painted whisk broom holder, 8 3/8" H x 4 1/2" W. $60
Right: Hand burned, painted and bejeweled whisk broom holder. This lady doesn't look as if she does much sweeping! Stamped Flemish Art Co. #605. $100

112

113

114

115

And So To Bed

116) This dresser set is lovely, lovely, lovely and very hard to find, especially in good condition. The burning and painting are both wonderful. The tray is 13" L x 9¾" W, and underneath is a paper label instructing: "Polish pyrocraft frequently with White Cherry Blossom Boot Polish. Finish with medium stiff brush."
$365

117) Hand mirrors were put out by all the major companies and were probably all imported from France as they made a "big deal" of the mirror being French bevelled plate glass.
Left: Gibson type, hand burned and painted, 8⅝" L x 4⅝" W. $95
Right: Muccha type, hand burned and painted, 13¼" L x 6¾" W. $180

118) Left: Poinsettias and leaves, hand burned and painted 7½" L x 4⅝" W. $95
Right: Flowers and leaves, burned but not painted, 10" L x 7" W. $125

119) Poinsettias and leaves hand burned and painted mirror, beautifully done. The photograph doesn't do this piece justice. The box is incredible on its own with red silk lining and silver and autumnal leaves adorning the outside. That it has survived all these years is a miracle! Mirror is 10⅛" L x 6" W. $225

116

117

118

119

You Name It, There Was A Box For It!

120) Three handkerchief boxes. Each one is well burned on all sides with good contrast, not painted. The one shown to top right is unmarked the other two are Flemish Art Co. #688. $65 each

121) Left: Burned and painted with yellow rose. Flemish Art Co. #688, $6^{5/8}$" x $5^{3/4}$", price $1.50 on bottom. You should be so lucky. $85
Middle: Burned and painted with cherries, $6^{1/4}$" x $5^{3/4}$", Flemish Art Co. #688. $85
Right: Burned and painted with red rose, $6^{3/8}$" x $5^{3/4}$" Flemish Art Co. #688. (Over twenty versions of style #688 exist.) $85

122) Handkerchief Box, Indian Chief. Burning includes nice pepper background work, 7" x 7", Flemish Art Co. $100

123) Handkerchief Box, Woman side face, the coloring makes this piece live. Crimson velvet lining. Flemish Art Co. #688. $85

124) Men's Handkerchief Boxes;
Left: Burned and painted with a pair of dogs to center, 6" x 6". $90
Middle: Stamped but hand painted with small oval scenes of country and sea and poinsettias, on hinges, PAT. MAY 6-16, 3/8" x $6^{3/8}$" $60
Right: Burned and painted with a stag in center of lid, $6^{1/4}$" x $5^{3/4}$", Flemish Art Co. #688. $90

120

121

122

123

124

125) Handkerchief boxes as Christmas gifts;
Top left: Stamped and hand painted, 5⅝" x 5¾", corner hinges stamped L.F. Grammes & Sons, Allentown, PA. $60
Top right: Stamped and hand painted, 6¾" x 6¼", stamped H.W.S. in design and Pat. Nov. 9-15 on hinges. $70

Bottom left: Hand burned and painted, pink lawn lining to inside bottom. Flemish Art Co. #688, 6¼" x 5⅞". $85
Bottom right: Stamped and hand painted, wizard hinges 6¼" x 5" $70

126) More handkerchief boxes - and we thought we were the only generation with allergies!
Top left: Stamped and hand painted with Poppies, signed on bottom R.L. H., 6¾" square. $70
Top right: Stamped and hand painted with daisies and bow, 5⅝" x 5½", Wizard hinges. $65
Bottom left: Stamped and hand painted, 6⅜" x 5⅜". $55
Bottom right: Stamped and hand painted yellow daisies and lady, WHS in design and Wizard hinges, 6½" square. $70

127) Boxes Showing Relief Burning
Left: Handkerchief box, a good example of relief burning, so well done it looks carved, hand painted flowers. $120
Center: Trinket box, semi relief burning and hand painted, 4½" x 3½". $50
Right: Trinket box with semi relief burning, painted, 4½" x 3½". $50

128) Two boxes by A.H. Balliet of Allentown, PA that were probably sold filled with candy as gifts. The top box, 6" x 3½" is open to show that the inside of factory stamped boxes often repeated the design on the outside. Bottom box 7¾" x 3½" both hand colored. $70 each

129) Top left: Stamped rose, grapes and orange design, not painted. Ink stamp on underside 2prs. Men's 1/2 Hose Size 10½". Socks or ties perfect presents for dad. 7½" x 4½". $25
Top right: Same box as top left but this has been hand painted, underside is stamped 2prs Men's 1/2 hose size 11. $70
Bottom: Stamped and hand painted with a delightful coastal view. Underside is ink stamped 9½ 2pr Men's Hose. Also 7½" x 4½". Maybe a standard size for socks boxes? $85

125

126

127

128

129

130) Top left: Stamped and hand painted, with Wizard hinges, back marked The D.L. Clark Co. Makers of fine confections, McKeesport, PA. 7 3/4" x 3 7/8". $85
Bottom left: Stamped and hand painted, side face of a woman. Written on bottom in pencil "A Merry Christmas Edith Malves." 6 3/8" x 3 3/8". $70
Right: Stamped and hand painted woman and horse, on bottom ink stamp 600 1/2 doz. (but what?) 9 3/8" x 6 1/2". $70

131) Top: Stamped and hand painted gift box nicely done, hinge stamped Box Mfrs. PLATT-MASCHER CHICAGO, 12" x 5 5/8". $80

132) Flatware Presentation box, stamped and hand painted with purple lining, one drawer and a lift top compartment. Made for William Rogers Silverware. A wedding gift? 9 1/8" x 10 1/2" x 4 5/8". $195

133) Top: Stamped and hand painted children's pencil box with three dividers inside, nice Bear, Deer and Fox on lid. 8" x 2 3/4". $70
Bottom: Stamped and hand painted pencil box showing children playing. 5 7/8" x 2 1/2". $80
Not too many pyrography items made for children survive - who would have known!

134) Left: Photograph box stamped and hand painted. $50
Center: Post Card box stamped and painted red Dutch children. $55
Right: Trinket box, stamped and hand painted with red rose and leaves. $40

130

132

131

133

134

96

135) Left: Gift or Candy box, stamped and hand painted. $50
    Right: Work Box stamped and hand painted, hinge marked Pat Nov. 9-15. $60

136) Top: Photo or Work Box stamped and hand painted, 9" x 4". $50
    Bottom: Utility box stamped and hand painted with WHS in design and pat. Nov. 8-15 on hinge 10 5/8" x 5 1/4". $60

137) Tie Boxes were used to store ladie's hair ribbons, not men's ties. The two at the top have identical stamping but have been painted different colors. Each is 11 1/4" x 3 1/2". $80
    Bottom: This has nicer stamping and is hand painted, written on the underside "Helen Mosers Christmas present.." 11 3/4" x 3 3/4". $80

138) Gloves were a big fashion item and a box kept them nice between social events.
    Left: Stamped design and hand painted 11 3/4" x 3 3/4". $60
    Top right: Daisies design is embossed with yellow paint accents to flowers and leaves. 10 3/8" x 3 5/8". $70
    Bottom right: Stamped and hand painted with pretty carnations of various colors trademark WHS stamped on lid. 10 1/4" x 3 1/2". $80

139) Glove boxes Flemish Art Co. #681 with three different treatments.
    Top left: Hand burned and painted with Morning Glory. $90
    Top right: Hand burned and painted in oils, beautiful roses. $110
    Bottom: Burned to perfection, not painted, blue silk lining. $85

135

136

138

137

139

140) Top: Hand burned and painted, Flemish Art Co. #681. At least 20 different designs were made with this
            model #. This box also has pyrography inside. $95
     Bottom: Bold design, pyrography and painting, lined with red silk, 11 3/4" x 4 1/4". $100

141) Top: Lovely burning and painting with green damask lining. 10" x 4". $90
     Bottom: Another version of Flemish Art Co. #681, - Do you get the feeling every lady must have owned
            one? Dad got socks or ties, Mother got gloves or handkerchiefs. Burned and painted outside, more pyrography
            inside with red velvet lining on bottom. $85

142) Delicately burned and nicely painted. She has that ideal girl next door look. Signed on underside C. Heel
     Sept. 06, Flemish Art Co. #681. $110

143) Yet another Flemish Art Co. #681. Burned and painted with more pyrography on inside lid. Same back-
     ground as "the girl next door" but this 'gal' is gonna have a lot more fun! $120

144) Guess the Flemish Art Co. # on these?
     Two very different burning and painting treatments of the same design.
     Top: Pale pink rose, pale green leaves, all very dainty and light, has blue silk lining. $100
     Bottom: Same box, same size 11 3/4" x 4 1/4" but looks much heavier, pink silk lining. $90

145) Top: Yet another Flemish Art Co. #681, this has a grape design and the initials EME worked into the lid.
     All hand burned and painted. The stamp on the bottom indicates it was sold by L.B. Herr Bookseller,
     Lancaster, PA. $95
     Bottom: Strawberry design is slightly smaller, 11 1/2" x 3 3/4" all hand burned and painted. Note the
     different clasp design. $95

146) Top: This work box is decorated with a lovely roses design. Well burned and painted, signed on bottom
     H.A. M. 14.10.12 with a partial paper label underneath reading: . . . ASTINGS & MILLER, Cameras &
     Photo. Artists Materials, ... Sporting. $100
     Bottom: Dainty burning and striking painting make this box a winner. $85

140

141

142

143

144

145

146

147) Collar and cuff boxes for the business man.
   Left: Poinsettia design, hand burned and painted with red silk lining. 6" square, Flemish Art Co. #685.
   $125

   Right: 3 ply panel carved, burned and painted, Flemish Art Co. #685, 6" square. $125

148) Dresser Boxes for the lady of the house. Not easy to find today but popular for storing jewelry.
   Top: Beautifully burned with good contrast dresser box. These are extremely hard to find now, especially in good condition. $195
   Bottom: Lovely burning and painting makes this dresser box one of our favorites. $295

149) Powder box stamped and hand painted, very pretty and unusual, $8^{3/8}$" x $4^{1/4}$" $95

150) Left: Trinket box with nicely burned and painted cherries design, lined with blue silk, part of paper label on underside reads: ". .W OLDE." 7" x $6^{1/4}$". $145
   Right: This trinket box was probably made for a man (why else would you pick a knight's helmet design?), Hand burned and painted with grey/blue silk lining, $6^{3/4}$" square. $100

151) Photograph Box or work box well burned with good flowing design and hand painted. $145

147

148

149

150

151

152) Top left: Well burned and painted photo box with lovely trailing grape vines, 9⁷⁄₈" x 4³⁄₈". $125
    Bottom left: Again, nice trailing design with cherries, nice burning and painting. $125
    Right: This was probably bought as a blank box. The pattern of a young boy walking among flowers and leaves designed, burned and painted by the artist. It has a nice primitive feel to it. Signed on the underside "Marie B. Brubaker 1912." $145

153) Photograph Box lovely burning and super coloring to the flowers, signed on back A.G. F. Flemish Art Co. #1037, 15¹⁄₄" x 7⁷⁄₈". $180

154) Another lovely photograph box with good burning and color, Thayer & Chandler #PB273, 14¹⁄₂" x 10¹⁄₂". $170

155) Last of the boxes is the sewing box we purchased from an old estate in New England. But it 'feels' European not American. The burning is very formal and controlled. $95

152

153

154

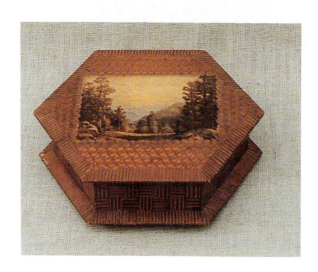

155

Burned Leatherwork

Our new Love?

156) For that special book in your life, a burned leather book cover with attached place marker, hard to find especially in this condition. $125

157) A selection of burnt leather photograph albums - excellent condition. These range in price from $65-85 depending on how well they are burned, if they are painted, and subject matter on the cover. You will come across quite a few inferior items. Don't even bother with them. They are not a good investment!
$65-85

158) Burnt leather novelties all in excellent condition;
Top left: Needle case in shape of a haystack. $60
Middle left: Double flap change purse. $40
Right: Teepee Calendar 1917. $40
Bottom: Leather sole shaped post card. Yes it was mailed. The address and stamp are on the back.
$20

159) Very rare burnt leather stereotypical black man with chicken poking from his bag. It is also painted. 11 1/2" H x 4 1/2" W. $200

156

157

158

159

160, 161, 162) Three Photographs showing a selection of leather and wood burned postcards. Postcards are not expensive and may be bought for $8 upwards from many postcard dealers. Guess they are not into leather! However, the price will rise accordingly depending on condition and subject matter. Expect to pay more for "Black" memorabilia, Indians, Patriotics, Bears, cards with inserts, or flaps with a message under and "saucies."
$8 and up

160

161

162

108

163) We saved the best for last. This is an exceptionally rare burned and painted skin. A wonderful piece. You have read the book. You decide what it is worth.

    We would like to leave you with its wistful message:
        So send me away with a smile, little girl
        Brush the tears from eyes of brown
        It's all for the best and I'm off with the rest
        Of the boys from my own home town,
        It may be forever we part, little girl,
        And it may be for only a while
        But if fight dear we must in our Maker we trust,
        So send me away with a smile.

    We hope he made it back and we hope you now have, if not a burning passion for American pyrography, at least a smoldering desire.

                                                                CAROLE AND RICHARD SMYTH

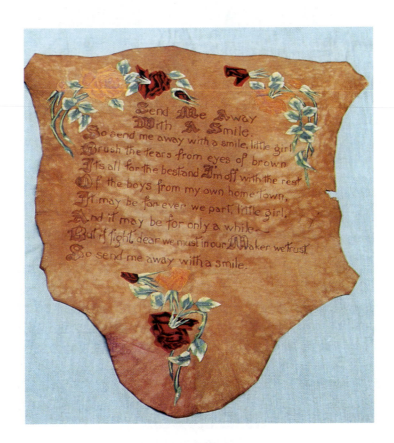

163

FURNITURE OF THE ARTS & CRAFTS PERIOD
"STICKLEY"
LIMBERT, MISSION OAK, ROYCROFT, FRANK LLOYD WRIGHT, AND OTHERS
WITH PRICES

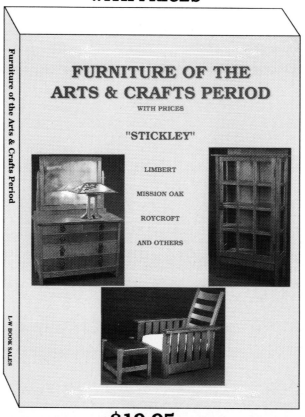

$19.95

This book has all of the leading manufacturers of Arts & Crafts Furniture of the early Nineteenth-Century. In this book are chairs, tables, settles, beds, magazine racks, bookcases, desks, cabinets, dressers, pedestals, tabourettes, etc. This book will be the book pricing Arts & Crafts Furniture. All prices are actual auction prices that these items have sold for. This book is a must for any Arts & Crafts Furniture collector or anyone just starting in the field.

156 pages + 4 pages of Color, PB, 8 1/2" x 11"

Send Check or Money Order + $2.00 Shipping for the first book and .30 for each additional book to:

L-W Book Sales
P.O. Box 69
Gas City, IN 46933

Or Call 1-800-777-6450 for Visa and Mastercard Orders Only!!

EARLY AMERICAN ANTIQUE COUNTRY FURNISHINGS

George C. Neumann
Item #1053

- Beds
- Chests
- Cupboards
- Desks and boxes
- Floor coverings
- Lighting
- Looking glasses
- Seating
- Tables and stands
- Timekeeping
- Cooking

- Woodenware
- Ceramic tableware
- Pewter
- Glassware
- Art
- Fabrics
- Personal articles
- Smoking
- Games and playthings
- Written documents

With more than 2100 photographed items from rarely seen private collections, this definitive encyclopedia of country furnishings covers the period from the 1600's, when early colonists were starting to make their own furnishings, to the 1800's, when patterns from centralized production began to fill American homes.

This volume has 354 pages, 8 1/2" x 11" softbound.

$19.95 + $2.00 Shipping
Send Check or Money Order To:
L-W Book Sales
P.O. Box 69
Gas City, IN 46933

Or Call **1-800-777-6450** for Visa, Mastercard and C.O.D. orders only!!!